Successful Private Practice in Neuropsychology

Successful Private Practice in Neuropsychology

A Scientist-Practitioner Model

Mary Pepping, Ph.D.

University of Washington
School of Medicine
and
Northwest Psychology Associates
Seattle, Washington

ACADEMIC PRESS

San Diego London Boston New York Sydney Tokyo Toronto

This book is printed on acid-free paper. ∞

Academic Press
An imprint of Elsevier
525 B Street, Suite 1900, San Diego, California 92101-4495, USA
http://www.academicpress.com

Academic Press
84 Theobald's Road, London WC1X 8RR, UK
http://www.academicpress.com

Library of Congress Catalog Card Number: 2003109373

International Standard Book Number: 0-12-551755-6

PRINTED IN THE UNITED STATES OF AMERICA
03 04 05 06 07 9 8 7 6 5 4 3 2 1

For my Parents, Elvira Dolly Pepping and John Joseph Pepping.

TABLE OF CONTENTS

5 A PRACTICAL GUIDE FOR OPENING YOUR BUSINESS

6 MARKETING AND OTHER MATTERS

7 CREATIVE APPROACHES TO FINANCIAL ISSUES

8 MEDICAL—LEGAL WORK

9 CONSULTATION AND SUPERVISION PRACTICE

10 PSYCHOMETRIC CONCERNS

11 TREATMENT PRACTICES FOR NEUROPSYCHOLOGISTS

12 NUTS AND BOLTS OF YOUR EVALUATION PRACTICE

13 HOW TO DESIGN AND IMPLEMENT A COGNITIVE GROUP

14 RESEARCH AS A DAILY REALITY

15 SUMMARY AND CONCLUSIONS

APPENDICES

FOREWORD

In 1993, after many years of work in institutional settings I decided to enter private practice and to become fully self-employed. Although I had a general sense of what would be required, it was only in day-to-day implementation of myriad clinical and business details over the next 6 years (as well as in trying to maintain some teaching and research interests) that I felt I learned most comprehensively what might constitute a good practice model.

I have designed this book to be a helpful guide for reviewing the issues and meeting the challenges of self-employment as a neuropsychologist, regardless of your particular clinical, research or teaching interests. This book will help practitioners who want to establish a practice, those who have been in practice for a few years and want to expand or refine their business, as well as those seasoned practitioners who simply wish to compare notes with another experienced neuropsychologist.

Psychology graduate students, interns and postdoctoral fellows exploring career options may find it helpful to learn more details about private practice here than they are likely to learn within the walls of academia. Psychologists of all stripes, even those employed in institutional settings, are likely to find portions of this book that could be implemented at their place of work, to maximize quality of work life there.

The conversational tone of the book is intended to allow the kind of open-minded review of ideas that leads to effective brain-storming and business development. This book also necessarily reflects my own approach to the topic of neuropsychological practice in general, and private practice in particular. There are many additional viewpoints, and I encourage you to find and consider them.

Three caveats:

This book is not intended as a primer on how to become a neuropsychologist. Those basic criteria are well described both in the National Academy of Neuropsychology's definition of what constitutes a neuropsychologist, and in the requirements for candidacy that are listed as part of the neuropsychology diplomate processes.

Nor is this book intended as a primer on how to create or conduct a forensic practice. While the medical-legal work described here can be an interesting, challenging and satisfying source of work for private practitioners, the skills you need to develop for that work go beyond the intent of this book.

Finally, while I discuss billing procedures, potential tax deductions, or other business matters, these represent my opinions, and should not be construed as legal advice. You need to determine what is appropriate for your own practice and then assure yourself that it conforms to local, state and federal laws.

People enter private practice for a variety of reasons. I did so to increase control of my work hours and daily schedule, clinical emphasis, and patient mix. While I had enjoyed a busy and varied psychotherapy practice for 15 years, I felt it was time for a break from that intense involvement in another person's intrapsychic life. I preferred not to have the daily responsibilities of an individual psychotherapy practice. I also wanted to shift my practice emphasis from its 60/40 neuropsychology/general clinical mix to an exclusively neuropsychological emphasis in my private practice.

When I started working as a self-employed person, I created a neuropsychological evaluation and consultation practice. In this practice, I evaluated patients, met with them and their families to review evaluation results and then referred them to the various outpatient therapies they needed, such as psychotherapy, speech therapy, vocational help. Although I had thorough contact with each patient during the evaluation and treatment planning phase, and typically performed most of the testing myself, I was not involved in the delivery of daily treatment activities that required my on-going presence. It was easier for me to achieve an enjoyable and productive balance of clinical work, teaching or writing, and research projects when I wasn't scheduled to see patients or supervise staff every day.

I also designed an actual 4-day work week that didn't simply stretch to accomplish 5 days work in the 4 days. I was able to decide which days of the week I would see patients, and which days I would reserve for paperwork, teaching, or other professional and personal activities. And I didn't have to take on other colleagues' workloads at various times throughout the year, when they were on vacation, out sick, or at conferences.

I was amazed at how simple it became to schedule a dentist appointment or other personal appointments. It no longer required the orchestration and long-term planning often required when working full-time in an institution. And I could run errands at a time of day that didn't involve weekend traffic and crowds. With this flexibility came a reduced amount of work commute in a city–Seattle–whose traffic problems are becoming increasingly renown.

In private practice, I also found that it was far easier to protect large blocks of time for record review, test data review, report preparation, journal reading, or for various writing projects, than it had been in a clinic setting. Settling down without interruptions to dictate reports improved the efficiency of my report preparation. I also had more space in which to work than the typical institutional office provides. And, if I wanted to take a break by taking a walk around the block to clear my mind and realign my posture, no one would look askance at this clear departure from clinic or departmental protocol.

The great irony for me in all this was that I had more time in which to develop my professional craft as a neuropsychologist when I was no longer in an institutional setting. The bulk of the work on this book and other academic writing and research projects were undertaken as part of my private practice.

A further irony is that while happily ensconced in my private practice, I was approached during the summer of 1999 by colleagues at the University of Washington School of Medicine (UWMC) and offered a full-time faculty position in the Rehabilitation Medicine Department. The new position was an intriguing one to me; I was asked to direct and expand the neuropsychology testing service as well as the outpatient neuro-rehabilitation treatment program. Both would involve the chance to see some additional populations of neurologic patients that I did not typically encounter in my private practice and also to reconnect with an experienced multi-disciplinary brain injury treatment team.

So at the age of 49, I decided it would be a positive professional development to tackle this version of academic life. I was excited by the opportunity to apply entrepreneurial and private practice principles to finding creative solutions to systems issues that were known to impede the delivery of optimal clinical services. The position also gave me the chance to work closely with many talented faculty and clinicians I liked and respected.

One of the most important things I have learned from alternating between institutional life and private practice is, regardless of our work setting, we have more freedom to craft a practice that works well for us than we think we do. Although some jobs do not lend themselves to the flexibility I advocate in this book, it is equally true that those of us with a strong work ethic may find it difficult to even consider these kinds of changes. This may be for fear of being perceived as less than productive, as not carrying our own weight, or as somehow not being fully up to the task of working ourselves to death. There is a funny (and I don't mean humorous) unspoken competition in many institutions, about who is toughest when it comes to bearing unreasonable demands, and a subtle pecking order established on those principles. So, you may have some decisions to make about your own quality of life and career. To borrow a phrase from Winnicott, you can be "the good enough" neuropsychologist and find that a sufficiently meaningful, satisfying, and lucrative goal.

You can still play a satisfying role in evaluation, treatment, teaching, training and research projects, in both the private and institutional setting. You can maximize what is positive about each, and reduce what is negative about each form of employment. For me, after almost four years of intense full time work in an institutional setting, the need for regaining balance is asserting itself. A schedule that includes the very structured part-time work in my medical school setting with the more flexible hours in my private practice is ideal for me. It is my hope that this book can help you find the combination of activities that will provide you with satisfying work, good connections with colleagues, and equitable reimbursement.

I would like to publicly thank my family and friends, and the many teachers, colleagues, mentors, and patients, who have been so instrumental in my personal and professional development. I will spare you this list but now that this book is completed, will get those thank you cards and letters out where they belong.

I thank Nikki Levy, Executive Editor at Academic Press and Elsevier Science, who initiated this project, Barbara Makinster, Senior Development Editor who kept it moving, Molly Wofford, Senior Project Manager who made sure its final form was clear and readable, and Trevor Daul for his assistance with marketing. Thank you all for your patience and cooperative spirit throughout this lengthy process. Finally, but most importantly, I want to thank my husband, who has been a source of ongoing inspiration, delight, intellectual challenge and emotional support to me, at every phase of this book.

Mary Pepping, Ph.D.
Seattle, Washington
April 2003
mpepping@u.washington.edu

PREFACE

Here is a description of the overall logic and layout of the ensuing chapters.

Chapter 1 is an overview of the key issues and challenges that are inherent in private practice, with some suggested solutions. Chapter 2 is the equivalent of "get out while you still can," and goes into some detail about the more harrowing aspects of self-employment and how to mitigate them. Chapter 3 provides a further antidote to the difficulties discussed in chapter 2, by reminding you of all of the outstanding advantages of self-employment.

Chapters 4, 5, and 6 are about developing your own unique private practice. In Chapter 4, the initial survey of the various ways you could spend your work time allows you to evaluate and determine what you really like to do. Chapter 5 has practical suggestions on ways to start safely and gradually accrue contracts and other sources of paid employment. Chapter 6 discusses marketing; most particularly, how to take advantage of professional activities you already enjoy and transform them into marketing tools.

Chapter 7 looks more closely at the expense side of the business and suggests creative approaches to managing costs.

Chapters 8 and 9 are devoted to special topics (as is Chapter 13), looking first at medical-legal work (Chap. 8) and at consulting work (Chap. 9) as interesting sources of income. Chapter 13 is devoted to a hands-on discussion of how to develop and deliver a cognitive group, to pique your interest about considering group treatment formats as part of your practice.

Chapters 10 and 11 examine specific neuropsychological concerns, with an emphasis on the interview and testing process in Chapter 10. A review of the clinical nuts and bolts of running a practice are included in Chapter 11, which covers topics ranging from referral etiquette to billing and collections.

Chapter 12 explores ways to design a therapy practice in the context of various kinds of neuropsychological services. Chapter 13 provides a practical example of a group treatment. Even people who don't want to have an individual treatment practice may find the suggestions in Chapter 13 for group treatment of interest. One can use an educational model that is not primarily psychotherapeutic in nature, and run it much as a class or course for participants.

Chapter 14 describes ways to keep the scientist alive in your self-employment framework, through research and publication. Chapter 15 is a final set of comments and a summary of the major ideas presented in this volume.

The appendices were developed to provide you with practical examples of helpful forms that I have used in my practice over the years. These forms range from consent forms to information sheets for patients, as well good reference sheets for typical Current Procedural Terminology codes and diagnostic codes that are common in neuropsychological practice. In addition, you will find a sample outline and handouts for a cognitive group. You are welcome to use any and all of the appendix materials, as long as you credit this source, and do not sell or distribute these pages for profit.

1

THE CHALLENGE OF PRIVATE PRACTICE IN NEUROPSYCHOLOGY

Overview of Key Issues and Effective Solutions

PROS AND CONS OF THE INSTITUTIONAL SETTING

One of the major challenges in a scientist-practitioner model of private practice is to preserve what is best about the academic and clinical aspects of full-time institutional work, while reducing the less attractive features such employment can bring.

On the positive side of the ledger, institutions such as hospitals, clinics, or universities typically provide an array of supports for their professional staff. This usually includes a regular salary, office space, transcription support, scheduling help, at least some built-in referrals from other departments, and billing and collections personnel. Paid sick leave and vacation days and perhaps some financial support for continuing education are also part of the package. In addition, one may have on-site opportunity for grand rounds or other in-service training. Finally, regular contact with like-minded colleagues can provide very helpful interpersonal and professional support and stimulation.

On the negative side of the ledger, one may be subject to an unreasonable workflow of patients that the institution has made a commitment to serve, but for whom sufficient clinical personnel have not been hired.

You may have very little control in the patient selection process (e.g., if patients are part of that system and need to see a neuropsychologist, you will see them). You may also be subject at times to the political vagaries of unfit or limited administrators or supervisors, to bureaucratic inefficiencies that affect daily quality of work life, or with unhelpful support staff. And there may not be a fair linkage between your level of productivity and your salary, nor, perhaps, room to grow and advance within your profession.

In the scientist–practitioner model for private practice in neuropsychology, you can thoughtfully plan work to create a career life that incorporates some of the best features of each world—the institutional and the self-employed. This approach allows for an ongoing refinement of your activities, in a manner that hopefully avoids or reduces some of the more egregious effects of bureaucracies and institutions and that offsets some of the negative aspects of private practice.

One way to maximize what institutions have to offer is to select an institution and department that you like and to negotiate a part-time contractual relationship with them (see chapters 4 and 5 for more details). In this manner, you may be able to see patients who would not typically come to your private practice, but whose neurologic problems may be of strong interest to you. You can also simply charge an hourly fee to the facility, and let it handle the billing and collections issues.

MAINTAINING HIGH-LEVEL SKILLS

When opportunities for continuing education are not built into your daily routines (such as stopping by grand rounds, attending the weekly brain cutting in neuropathology, listening to the neuroradiologists debate the merits of particular imaging approaches or neuroanatomic details of an interesting case), you need to find solid and creative ways to fill this gap. Neuropsychologists must not neglect to update and expand their knowledge in the areas of neuroanatomy, neuropathology, and basic neurobehavioral issues associated with various diseases and syndromes, once they have graduated from formal training. Although annual professional conferences and journal articles help, there is nothing like observation and discussion with expert colleagues to promote new growth in our own neuronal systems.

You may need to expand or supplement your reading of professional journals and develop a regular journal club meeting with colleagues. These activities can expose you to new knowledge and help ensure that you regularly hear informed perspectives on professional matters. Two helpful avenues for ongoing development of your skills include reviewing specific cases with other neuropsychologists who may have special areas of interest or developing an ongoing consultation relationship with a more experienced neuropsychologist.

Attending local meetings of your community's neuropsychology and neurology society meetings can be an excellent source of up-to-date clinical and research information and a potential source of referrals. These two groups can be particularly important for neuropsychologists, who need to be at the top of their form with respect to specific testing knowledge and broader neurobehavioral issues. The latter includes adequate understanding of the disease or injury from a medical standpoint, especially as it is likely to affect neuropsychological functions.

There are also workshops, conferences, new books, and new test training opportunities. Although one may need to be selective, sharing the cost and use of these resources can be a very helpful approach in private practice. Books and test materials may be loaned to colleagues in similar circumstances. For some conferences, you and your colleagues may decide to rotate attendance, with the attendee prepared to bring back specific ideas, reprints, and tapes to share.

It is important to acknowledge that scientist-practitioners in private practice are often caught between their training needs and the time and cost associated with leaving one's practice to pursue such opportunities. When we fly to a conference, give a talk, or attend a workshop, we not only bear the full training expense, but we must also continue to cover our rent and other overhead, while not earning any income during the time we are away. I am not sure if that constitutes a triple whammy, or merely a double whammy, but it is one of the more challenging aspects of self-employment.

Fortunately, a sole proprietor can keep an income stream flowing, by hiring neuropsychologists to conduct evaluations in your absence, in a manner prenegotiated with some of your referral sources (see Chapter 7). And, if one implements some of the cost-sharing ideas described above for continuing education needs, you will find a stimulating and satisfying mix of information that doesn't break the bank in the process. Finally, the heightened awareness, thoughtfulness, and energy that private practitioners must invest in their own training can produce a level of development in one's own craft not always found among personnel more safely ensconced in an institutional setting.

THE INTERDISCIPLINARY NETWORK

For me, the most difficult aspect of private practice was the loss of an established and mature interdisciplinary team for the comprehensive evaluation and treatment of neurologically compromised patients. (Such a team typically includes speech therapy, occupational therapy, physical therapy, vocational counseling, physiatry and social work.) This has been especially true for those patients of working age, for whom well-integrated team treatments are often critical if they are going to resume competitive employment and reestablish a more normal life of work, love, and play.

My neuropsychological evaluation can certainly document the patient's cognitive, emotional, characterologic, and neurobehavioral disturbances and strengths, and I can make recommendations for further work-up by other disciplines. It is a source of concern and frustration at times, however, to witness the sort of piecemeal and poorly integrated help some of these patients will receive because their various practitioners are scattered throughout the city. There is often no clear case manager and no good forum for effective communication among providers.

Perhaps this varies significantly from city to city throughout the United States and Canada, or it may be different in other countries. In America, it seems relatively easy to find similar practitioners self-employed together (e.g., physicians, psychologists, neuropsychologists, speech pathologists, or vocational counselors), but more difficult to find self-employed interdisciplinary groups who provide comprehensive outpatient neurorehabilitation services.

A number of approaches can be helpful in this circumstance. One obvious solution is to form good working relationships with as many of the various institution-based and private outpatient programs in the larger community as possible. One further advantage to starting out in an institution or program prior to becoming self-employed is that you have firsthand appreciation for the respective strengths and limitations of each program. You can then more effectively direct your own patients to programs likely to meet their treatment needs.

It is also possible to develop good working systems with therapists from various private practices who get to know one another over time through you and through patients that you have sent them to treat. It is important in this circumstance to make sure that someone has been designated as the clinical team leader. Sometimes the attending physician capably fills this role alone; at other times, an experienced rehabilitation therapist or neuropsychologist may need to monitor all of the treatment elements. This function of team leader in monitoring treatment is another practice option for the neuropsychologist.

In addition, the newly self-employed neuropsychologist could certainly learn from experienced private nurse case managers and private vocational rehabilitation counselors. They have typically developed extensive and reliable networks of interdisciplinary colleagues. They know firsthand the potential pitfalls of fractionated care for neurologically compromised patients, who are usually not able to function effectively as their own case managers.

DO NOT GO GENTLY INTO THAT RESEARCH DECLINE

While you are busily evaluating an increasing flow of interesting patients, you may think it unlikely to have time for research. Yet one of the ironies of private practice may be that you actually have more time and freedom with which to explore research questions than when you were pushed for higher and higher clinical productivity in an institutional setting whose overhead costs demand immense levels of productivity from clinicians.

Once again, both good planning and a willingness to think outside of the box can be critical for good research. First of all, establish a good data summary sheet, including demographics, and make sure you complete it for each patient. This will not only support your clinical efficiency (dictating reports is easier when following a certain format and this allows you to easily send specific test scores when requested by other psychologists), but it also gives you a good basic working variable list for data entry. (In addition to a good data summary sheet, a good referral log will prove invaluable. See chapter 6.)

Although the tests you use in any given evaluation may vary somewhat, are there core instruments you are likely to use consistently across most evaluations? Does current research in your populations of interest (e.g., Alzheimer's patients, multiple sclerosis patients, mildly head-injured patients) suggest that there are key neuropsychological variables to monitor? Are you curious to see how comparatively new instruments (e.g., subtests of the Wechsler Memory Scale-III) might compare to older instruments, in a way that is both clinically relevant and heuristically useful?

Local graduate students looking for thesis or dissertation opportunities may be happy to help set up, enter, and analyze your data if in return they can have access to a particular subset of the information for their project. You can easily keep a master, secured list of patient names and simply enter numbers on the data summary sheet to protect patient identity, but otherwise the graduate student has access to pertinent information.

You can also incorporate an annual review of such research questions and data collection by linking it to something essential, such as end-of-the-year final tax preparation. This data-collection template review can also be part of your journal club discussion with colleagues, to determine if people are willing to collect information in comparable formats and to have a shared database for particular populations, or other variables.

CREATING EDUCATIONAL OPPORTUNITIES

In addition to the suggestions listed under Maintaining High Skill Levels, you may wish to consider the following:

1. If you were institution based at some point in your immediate past, or if you have a colleague who is, request permission to attend an in-house conference or two, such as weekly neuroradiology rounds or neuropathology brain cuttings. In addition, sitting in on a neuroanatomy or

neuropathology seminar can be a helpful source for both review and consolidation of basic science information.

2. Many departments have lectures that are open to all interested professionals. Simply checking a web site may provide you with the lecture schedule.

3. Pursuing adjunct clinical faculty status at a local institution can bring with it teaching and clinical supervision opportunities, as well as collaborative research projects, likely to provide impetus for continued reading, thinking, and lecturing.

4. If adjunct clinical faculty appointments are not an option, offer to be a guest lecturer for a neuropsychology topic in a colleague's course. This is another good way to gain entry into the system.

5. Submitting workshop ideas or participating in presentations on a regular basis at professional conferences is an obvious but sometimes overlooked option for private practitioners. You may have an interesting series of case studies that would challenge an existing research finding or that would extend our understanding of a neuropsychological issue. It would also be a good forum for presenting the results of your data collection, e.g., comparison of patients' performances on two tests measuring verbal memory.

PRODUCTIVELY MANAGING ANXIETY: INCOME

One of the best ways I have found to reduce anxiety about paying the bills and making a living in the ebb and flow of private practice is to create a combination of both guaranteed and more flexible income sources. (See Chapter 7 for more detailed financial advice and Chapter 4 for practice details.) In my case, I started out with two established contracts, each on a part-time basis, one with a small nonprofit medical clinic and one with a private rehabilitation company. The former contract averaged about 12 hours work per week, the latter ranged from a minimum of 5 hours up to 20 hours in any given month. The combined total income provided a bedrock of support, regardless of the vagaries of time, changes in referral sources, managed care, or patient flow.

In addition to this, cultivating private practice referrals with self-insured companies, or as part of independent medical exams (IMEs), can provide well-reimbursed and reliable income. The evaluation has been preauthorized by the referring person prior to your appointment with the patient, you are typically provided with the name, address, and number of the person to be billed, and you do not have to spend your time on hold, calling a 1-800-number, and trying to deal with an 18-year-old "insurance specialist" following an aggravating menu of responses to requests for preauthorization or for payment.

You may also wish to join resources with other neuropsychologists and help to hire someone skilled at preauthorization, billing, and collections. Or you may wish to pay a psychometrist an additional fee to do preauthorization on an interim basis until your practice can afford to make these external arrangements.

Private practitioners can also organize remunerative workshops. These workshops often provide multiple direct and indirect benefits: income and marketing, introductions to local colleagues, and development of your teaching skills. In addition, if you live in a city that has widespread appeal at particular times of the year (e.g., Phoenix in the winter, Seattle in the summer), this location has an added appeal for practitioners wishing to combine professional leave and training with vacation time.

Over time you may have accumulated many patients with a particular problem that might interest other psychologists as a workshop topic. For example, the neuropsychological effects of electrical injuries constitute a very interesting syndrome, yet most clinicians do not have a large number of these patients in their practices.

You may also have a particular teaching interest (e.g., ethical dilemmas in neuropsychology) that might draw a good number of participants. You could teach independently or in cooperation with your state psychology association's continuing education program, provided to members at a fee.

PROTECTIVELY MANAGING ANXIETY: MALPRACTICE

The best way to manage potential malpractice problems is to prevent them. Although you should be appropriately insured, it is equally important that you practice only within your areas of expertise. A series of workshops in neuropsychology does not constitute adequate specialty training, nor does simply being trained to administer neuropsychological tests. Although both of these activities may constitute valuable aspects of your training, they are not adequate training for a neuropsychologist.

None of us is perfect, and we all need to be vigilant about our procedures and conclusions. All of us, even the most experienced neuropsychologist, should have consultation with colleagues as a routine part of our practice, regardless of setting. This will also help manage malpractice anxiety and provide good objective support if it is needed to prove that you (a) consulted with others about questions or concerns in a given case, (b) were confirmed in your approach or conclusions, or (c) incorporated something into your approach that you might not have otherwise.

However, it has been my observation that the risk of missing something important in a patient's test presentation, whether an occult neurologic problem or a significant characterologic factor, is increased with a reduced amount of experience, and/or with less than intensive training in the specialty. If you don't meet the basic criteria for the profession, for example, as outlined by the National Academy of Neuropsychology to practice as a neuropsychologist, or the requirements to qualify as a candidate for board certification in neuropsychology, you should take the appropriate steps to remedy the missing items in your training. In the interim, you should probably not be independently conducting neuropsychological evaluations and reports, nor testifying as a neuropsychologist.

In addition to such basic professional qualifications, there are helpful guiding principles: Treat patients well. Write reports that are honest and respectful in tone and nature regardless of the findings. Make sure the patient understands the findings in a follow-up meeting when appropriate. Return phone calls as soon as possible. Let people know if there will be a delay in receiving a written report.

In addition, providing clear information about your practice, preferably in written documents such as a patient informed consent sheet, as well as an information sheet about your practice, your fees, hours, or philosophy, and keep everyone informed and appropriately directed (see Appendix C). In addition, for both you and the patient, this is a helpful reminder of the rights and limits that each person carries in the evaluation or treatment circumstance.

PERSONALITY FACTORS IN PRIVATE PRACTICE

Private practice is likely to be more satisfying than frustrating for you if you have an entrepreneurial spirit, are generally independent and self-directed, are energetic, and are willing to take on (or know how to delegate) a wide variety of clinical and business details. Being reasonably undefended and highly responsible, willing to listen to feedback of all kinds, and to take action to improve your process or product, are all important parts of running a successful independent practice.

A tolerance for risk, good ego strength, and an optimistic bent are all qualities I see when I observe practitioners who appear both successful and happy in their work. I also think it helps psychologically to know that there is a certain highly variable rhythm that seems to occur in private practice, with periods of being swamped by demands, periods of striking just the right balance, and periods of being uncomfortably not busy.

This is likely to be especially true in the first few years of getting started in your business, but can also occur from time to time in any well-established practice. Long-time referral sources may move or retire, policy changes may occur within local institutions where you have historically worked part-time, or contract needs for private companies may undergo major revisions in these times of increased health-care costs.

Being able to maintain a long-term perspective, to believe in your own skills and appeal, to seek feedback about possible problems in the practice or marketplace and respond accordingly are all important factors. In addition, remaining collegial and respectful of other neuropsychologists' rights to a differing opinion, avoiding being set up as legal enemies in the service of adversarial court proceedings involving shared patients, and appreciating that there may be more than one way of doing good work are all important characteristics in developing and maintaining a successful private practice.

EGO NEEDS AND DECREASED PRESTIGE

To some extent, meeting ego and prestige needs will depend upon what accomplishments you value and perhaps to some degree upon the opinions or shared values of the professional circles in which you travel. If making a good income is your primary goal, and you succeed in that area, the rest may be moot. If being invited to give workshops or lectures is important to you as an indicator of success, you will want to cultivate those activities.

A university affiliation as a part-time clinical or adjunct faculty member, in either an undergraduate institution or as part of a medical facility, may be an important feature of your identity and satisfaction. If having a primary association with a major organization, such as a clinic, medical school, hospital, or university is important to you, you may well be able to maintain that position and develop a part-time practice under institutional strictures and requirements. The guidelines in this book could also apply to the development and maintenance of that adjunctive type of practice.

I think it is possible to develop the kinds of clinical experiences, teaching portfolio, conference presentations, and publications that would support a private practice or nonacademic commitment to the scientist–practitioner model. There are a number of good working models for this combination in the neuropsychology world: Well-known individuals continue to write, publish, present, and teach and are not in formal academic settings. They also continue to see patients or direct clinical programs.

ONGOING CONSULTATION: ARE YOU WILLING TO SEEK IT? THE BUCK STOPS HERE

One of the best ways to prevent problems in your private practice is to seek regular consultation with more experienced colleagues. In some parts of the country, it is routine and expected for even experienced psychologists to regularly seek individual supervision or consultation. In some places of practice, a peer review group model is the most commonly used. (In such a circumstance, like-minded practitioners meet once a month to discuss concerns, and cases.) Some practitioners prefer to periodically call upon an individual consultant for a particular concern, question, or case.

Too often, in my experience, licensed practitioners do not seek regular consultation advice, fearing perhaps that it signifies inadequate knowledge or a failure of professional development. I think the opposite is true: The excellent practitioners are aware that they do not and cannot know it all and actively seek ways to review and improve their decisions, analyses, conclusions, behavior, and policies towards their patients and their practice. Even if you are the most experienced person in your community, there are colleagues in other states who would be glad to consult with you.

All psychology practitioners, including, and perhaps especially, neuropsychologists, who may not have experienced much, if any, intrapsychically-oriented work as part of their graduate, internship, and postdoctoral training with patients will benefit from personal experience as patients in the individual psychotherapy process. We all have our blind spots, our shadow side, our areas of cathexis, which can make a real difference to our perception of patients and their problems, both neurologic and otherwise.

For example, being aware of our own tendencies towards undue harshness of opinion, rigidity of thought, or our unconscious needs to function as saviors or advocates for patients, can be essential to proceeding with fairness and caution. This may be especially critical, in the murkier areas of differential diagnosis with patients who have complex preinjury or illness histories, in addition to their acquired or reactive problems.

So these are some foundational and theoretical reasons why we should all seek consultation. It is also worth remembering that when things go wrong in private practice, you do not have an institution and its resources to protect you. However, it has also been my observation that if things go wrong for staff within an institution, the kind of institutional support may be highly variable in its quality and effect. An institution's first order of business is to protect itself as an organization; protecting you as a member of the organization comes second.

Finally, people in private practice can select their own malpractice insurance group. You may prefer to do business with companies experienced with psychologists.

EXERCISE: IS PRIVATE PRACTICE REALLY RIGHT FOR YOU?

1. *Review the issues raised in this chapter and list the three areas of most immediate concern to you in pursuing a private practice.*

2. *Using a problem-solving approach like the ABODES system (see the Appendix J for Cognitive Group Handouts), list all of the possible solutions or avenues to explore in addressing your three concerns.*

3. *Gather all of the needed information on one of those three concerns, as if you were ready to make the move into self-employment. For example, maybe a major concern is being able to afford office space. Meet with as many private practitioners as you know and see how they have obtained space. Be willing to trade your time in testing someone else's patients in return for use of space and materials.*

4. *Does the information you are discovering make you excited to pursue self-employment, or does it make you feel tired and stressed? Does it all feel too burdensome and too much hassle, or do you feel energized by the possibilities? Those may be important early indicators to you about your comfort with full-time self-employment.*

2

OTHER POTENTIAL INDIGNITIES

At the end of Chapter 1, I asked the question, "Is private practice really right for you?" This was based in part upon a review of the challenges present in maintaining a scientist-practitioner model of self-employment as compared to other settings. The last chapter was also intended to help you think critically about what you want professionally and how to have more of what you want as an entrepreneur. I also touched briefly upon the personal interests and qualities likely to be important in maintaining satisfying self-employment.

In this chapter, I would like to take a cold, hard look at the costs, direct and indirect, of doing business on your own. If at the end of chapter 2, you are still interested in establishing a private practice, I think it is a sign that you and self-employment may well be meant for each other. You may then be living proof of P.J. O'Roark's contention in *Eat the Rich* that thriving economies are not so much a matter of political philosophy or a question of abundant natural resources. Instead, where there is freedom and rule of law, humans will prosper.

People in private practice may value freedom to do as they see fit under the rubric of basic professional guidelines as the most fundamental component of a happy life. It is worth the risk and the cost when one has the power to choose, act, and react with independence and not to spend one's valuable energies trying to push large rocks up insurmountable hills. Now, let's take a look at the hard realities of self-employment.

NO PAID SICK LEAVE OR HOLIDAYS

When you work for yourself, there is no professional or sick leave paid for by someone else. When you are ill, patients do not get seen, and you do not get paid. Further, there are no paid national holidays. When you go on vacation, you need to make arrangements for someone else to cover your practice or to close it down while you are gone. If taking call or being on call is an issue, you need to arrange with colleagues to rotate this responsibility.

NO ADDITIONAL REIMBURSEMENT FOR PROFESSIONAL FEES

Reimbursement for conference costs comes fully from your own pocket, unless you have been specifically hired to work at the conference for an honorarium or with expenses paid. Even if the work is invited and paid, it is not likely to cover the cost of what you would have earned had you stayed home and done several neuropsychological evaluations. You will also usually have continuing education requirements for your continuing state licensure, and you must pay out-of-pocket for completing those requirements.

NO GUARANTEED SALARY OR HEALTH CARE BENEFITS

You have no guaranteed salary and no built-in benefits, such as health insurance, dental insurance, matching funds for retirement, and other forms of reimbursement (e.g., cost of your license or of professional organizations). Such benefits typically constitute a value equal to an additional 20–25% of your base salary when you are employed by an institution or company.

As a sole proprietor, you usually need to pay for your health insurance and possibly your family's coverage as an individual and not as a member of a group. Hence you not only don't have subsidized health care, but the cost of the insurance you obtain costs far more than it costs people who are institutional employees. The same is typically true for disability insurance policies, which you can get cheaper as part of a group rate with your employer. Certainly professional organizations, such as the American Psychological Association (APA), may be able to provide some reasonable group policies in these benefit areas, but you are otherwise not subsidized by an employing organization.

OVERHEAD EXPENSES

All of the expenses of doing business are yours, including finding and leasing office space, hiring transcription or reception support, deciding who is going to do your scheduling and billing, buying or leasing your own waiting area furniture and office equipment, buying or sharing testing equipment, and developing and paying for letterhead, envelopes, and business cards. All mailing costs, copying costs, and supplies are your direct expense, as are telephones and voicemail systems. You will also spend time and money for marketing letters and materials. These are just the basic expenses in a relatively uncomplicated private practice.

BILLING, COLLECTIONS, AND TAXES

You may want to hire the assistance of psychometrists, as well as people to help with office billing and collections. There is likely to be significant paperwork to complete for managed care companies and insurance companies if you want to participate as a preferred provider. You will also have to complete documents justifying the request for testing in various circumstances. In the United States, you will also need to obtain city, county, or state business licenses, file quarterly taxes, pay local and state business taxes, and provide 1099 IRS information each year for any contract employees who earned more than $600 from you. You may decide that it makes sense for you to incorporate, in which case an accountant will be needed.

If you are still with me, I am happy to move on to Chapter 3, letting you know the good news and the possibilities involved in managing all these details. It will be useful for you, however, to first take a detailed look at your own personal balance sheet. Establish the net income required to support yourself and your family, along with anticipated overhead, and direct and indirect costs of doing business. If you are employed by an institution, or have that possibility as one of your current options, carefully compare the direct and indirect costs and benefits of each setting.

EXERCISE: PERSONAL BALANCE SHEET FOR DIRECT AND INDIRECT COSTS

1. *List all of the direct costs involved in establishing a private practice:*
   a. *Estimated office rent*
   b. *Malpractice insurance*
   c. *Test materials and other office supplies*
   d. *Furniture, prints, rugs, lamps*

   e. *Stationery, including announcements regarding your practice opening*
   f. *Open house or other marketing costs*
   g. *Office equipment, such as a computer, software, testing materials, and so on*
   h. *Support staff (e.g., billing, transcription, reception)*
   i. *Cleaning costs per week or month*
   j. *Telephones, voicemail services, pager, cell phone*
   k. *Other (e.g., licensure, professional organization dues, journal dues)*
2. *If you are currently institution-based, consider these indirect costs:*
   a. *If you are going to lose health insurance coverage, what will private insurance cost you and your family?*
   b. *How many paid vacation days and holidays do you have, and what dollar amount does that now represent?*
   c. *Does your current place of employment pay for professional leave, the costs of some conferences, or travel?*
   d. *Do you have matching funds for retirement at your place of employment? If so, how much will you lose by leaving? If you are already vested, what dollar amount would they have matched for future years of work?*

3

THE GOOD NEWS

There is much to love about private practice, and there are probably as many practitioners as there are reasons why people decide to take this step in their careers. Here is a partial listing of the factors many people find compelling and necessary at some stage in their professional development.

INTEGRATING SKILLS AND INTERESTS IN PATIENT SELECTION

Private practice offers a clear invitation to rethink all of your priorities, especially the nature, focus, and extent of your clinical activities. You may come to a point in your professional life when you would like to further develop a particular skill. For instance, you may want to enhance your individual treatment abilities, but there may not be the need nor opportunity for this shift in your current job. Perhaps you want to pursue further education in your field (e.g., complete another formal fellowship, pursue geriatric or rehabilitation training, or enter into psychoanalytic training). Entering private practice is an opportunity for promoting self-directed professional growth.

Even if the nature of your work suits and satisfies you, perhaps you would like to alter your particular patient mix, but that is not possible in your current work environment. I think the issue of patient mix (i.e., what sorts of illnesses or injuries or problems characterize the patients you serve) can be a particularly strong concern for neuropsychologists, because we see so many people with catastrophic injury or illness.

For example, much as you may have to offer, and as much as you may feel privileged to be at the side of some patients, years of watching people succumb in their 30s or 40s to malignant brain tumors can take its toll. Trying to comfort families where the wife and mother has sustained a severe traumatic brain injury, or watching people your age struggle with the increasing symptom load of virulent forms of multiple sclerosis can darken your worldview. It can also leach emotional energy needed for the quality of your own life, and that of your family and friends, in whatever time you have left on this planet.

In private practice, you can decide which groups of patients you will see and which you will refer to others. You can also design a practice that does not require emergency coverage, freeing you from obligation for weekends, suicidal patients, or too many people with Axis II disorders. One of the advantages of being experienced when you make a shift into self-employment is that you will have a better understanding of who you most enjoy seeing, what work you most enjoy doing, and some understanding of your own limitations and needs. With this self-knowledge to guide you, can begin to design a practice that is most likely to satisfy you.

CREATING THE OPTIMAL SCHEDULE

In private practice, how you structure your days is completely up to you. First you need to decide what relative percentage of evaluations, treatment, teaching, research, supervision, and "other" you would like to include in your professional practice. You will want to choose a mix of activities that is intrinsically interesting to you and that will also pay the overhead. And while you are at it, why don't you presume your initial plan is likely to undergo some evolution with increased opportunities?

I approached my private practice by setting up a .25 contract with a local private outpatient clinic, spending one full day a week on site conducting neuropsychological evaluations. I did my dictation from home via the clinic's telephone dictation system. I averaged about 12 hours a week in this position. Six of those hours were guaranteed whether patients showed up or not, so even if I had a no-show, income was not a total loss.

During my start-up phase, I also spent about 5 hours a week consulting with a private brain-injury rehabilitation company. I did this both onsite and in the community. My responsibilities included weekly case review, some staff training, consultation on neuropsychological, behavioral, and psychological concerns for patients, and participation in conferences held at patients' homes.

The next element of my initial practice template was to conduct one to two private neuropsychological evaluations per month for the first 6 months. Initially, I did no marketing other than word of mouth, and was content for the practice to build slowly (see Chapter 6 for more extensive advice on marketing). During this same time, I continued to teach one undergraduate psychology course at a private university, which I had begun for fun when I was working full-time in an institutional setting.

For me, the four elements of clinic work, private evaluations, consultation, and classroom teaching worked well as a leaping off point for self-employment. As my practice continued to build over time, I decided to redirect my teaching time and energy to periodic lectures at a medical school. I had discovered that carrying full responsibility for 30 undergraduates with term papers, midterms, finals, grades, and office hours on campus was ultimately not the best use of my time. I still miss those students, but now I enjoy teaching psychology and physiatry residents.

Flexible Hours and Days

I am sitting at my computer on a sunny afternoon midweek; the house is completely quiet. My golden retriever is snoozing with his muzzle resting on my slippers while the cat is draped lazily over the blanket at the top of his perch. I can actually think without phones ringing, faxes beeping, and overhead paging announcements echoing in the background. No one is knocking on my door and I have space and time in which to move and think. These are the splendid moments in a well-planned schedule.

So, how do you decide how to arrange your hours and days in a workable, efficient, and restorative pattern? Some practitioners schedule all of their patient contact and clinical work into three comparatively long days with no patient contact on the remaining two. Others find that a Monday through Thursday schedule works well, and they take Fridays off, creating a 3-day weekend every week. If you have the support of a good psychometrist or two in your practice, you may be able to spend mornings interviewing patients, reviewing records, returning phone calls, doing dictation, catching up on correspondence, and save every afternoon for nonclinical activities.

If you have young children, you may need to do some negotiating with your spouse or baby-sitters to arrange times during the week when the children are not on the premises. Even if it is only for a 2- or 3-hour increment once or twice a week, you will be astonished at what you can accomplish when the push is on, and quiet, protected time is yours. After a while, the cadence of this routine will help you be extremely efficient and prepared to settle down to work quickly (e.g., for a stint of focused dictation of reports).

First Choice on Vacation Slots

One major advantage of self-employment is that you can decide when you wish to be away from the office and you can arrange your schedule accordingly. Especially if you have an evaluation and consultation practice that does not include psychotherapy, it is relatively easy to schedule blocks of time when you plan to be away.

Prior to launching into private practice, I knew I wanted the flexibility to travel even after I returned to work. Developing a taste for travel or other important avocational pursuits provides a strong incentive for making life outside of work happen now, rather than waiting for the time and space to somehow happen on their own. They usually won't happen on their own. A life of indentured servitude to the priorities of work is not one most of us would consciously choose. But this can be a particularly dangerous liaison if you love your work.

Fortunately, neuropsychologists are in a unique position among psychologists in a clinical practice, since our work tends to be time-limited. Although it may be intensive and time consuming, cases are typically brought to completion relatively quickly. Once the report and recommendations are completed, we can move on to other cases. While we remain available for further discussion in any given case, we do not typically have to carry on-going requirements for someone's care.

Professional Activities

When you have the flexibility of self-employment, you may design contracts for varying durations—a year or a semester—and remain available to an interesting variety of other employment options. This kind of access to life's opportunities is very difficult to achieve while working within an institution, which is by nature both less flexible in options and more fixed in routines. In the institution's necessary attempts to manage a large, complex set of intersecting needs and requirements, a degree of negative influence and demand can be unfairly placed upon employees. The net result is fewer degrees of freedom and, often, built-in bias or unfairness in how assets or supports will be distributed. By contrast, the solo practitioner is usually far better able to track billing and collections, more free to negotiate contracts and responsibilities than is true in most institutions.

In private practice, you can consciously and freely create a template for your professional activities that includes part-time commitments you don't wish to change and part-time activities that are meant to evolve. With managed care and cost cutting, opportunities for self-employment or contract work in institutional settings have actually increased, not decreased. If there is a particular organization or program that you like, you may be able to negotiate an attractive contractual arrangement. Although they will probably not guarantee longevity of the work, you may develop an interesting combination of patients and colleagues during the time you work with them.

Finally, private practitioners need not have all their financial eggs in one basket. When you survey your professional activities, keep this important thought in mind: If your current company or institution decides to downsize, you may have very little control over your own job's survival, no matter how dedicated and valued you have been. There are usually no such unpleasant surprises in private practice, and you are the person in charge of allocating duties and assets.

SETTING YOUR OWN FEES

I have worked for companies I thought charged too little for my time, and I have worked for companies that I thought charged too much. In one circumstance, we were in danger of being a dumping ground for patients with little to no insurance coverage for neuropsychological evaluations. In the other circumstance, I was hard-pressed to explain to private nurse case managers why my employer felt the need to charge $50 more an hour for each hour of an evaluation than did comparably experienced neuropsychologists in the community.

It was a distinct pleasure to me to be able to set my own fees, which I did by considering three primary factors (see Chapter 7 for more details):

1. What were the range of fees in the local market?
2. How did my level of experience and expertise compare to that of all other established neuropsychologists in the area?
3. What fee will properly acknowledge and compensate my work and will be a good value for referral sources?

DETERMINING SALARY

When I first began my private practice, I wanted to be able to gross $75,000 to $80,000 a year, and to keep expenses to an absolute minimum. I figured I could do this with 20 hours per week of fee-for-service work, with a combination of direct clinical time, consultation time, and medical-legal case review. During my first year of practice I made about $50,000, but I was not fully busy. By the second year, I was regularly filling my private evaluation slots, and I was easily generating $75,000 to $80,000 a year, with the equivalent of half-time clinical work.

You may have a good sense of what income you and your family need. You need to be sure, in a self-employment model, to include money for overhead and benefit costs. If you have a working spouse who can include you on his or her insurance plan, so much the better. My husband and I were both self-employed at the time I embarked upon private practice, so we carried all of our own overhead costs.

In private practice, you can more clearly determine what you need, what you want, and how to arrange your time and energy to make that happen, with significant control over the outcome.

CHOOSING YOUR OWN SUPPORT SERVICES

Another advantage of a solo private practice is that you can personally choose and hire the people who will provide your support services. This may be simply a terrific medical transcriptionist and a good courier service (to deliver those dictated tapes and reports). Or you may one day have a full complement of front and back office staff for reception, billing and collections and clerical support as you pool resources with other private providers. Finding and hiring good people for these positions can be challenging but satisfying, and you have far more control over who is hired, and who works for you than in an institutional setting. I feel I have been very lucky in all of the institutions where I have worked, because I have always had good support staff.

That is not always the case, however, and having less than optimal support staff is a regular complaint among some of my colleagues in other settings. A rude receptionist, a transcriptionist who can't spell, a secretary who is interested in doing only the absolute minimum required to keep the job, or a scheduler who feels it is his job to provide unasked for psychotherapy over the phone to potential patients, do not promote the kind of positive working environment you want for your patients and your referral sources. In many settings, there is not much you can do about these problems. In private practice, you can.

OFFICE LOCATION, SPACE, AND ATMOSPHERE

In the institutional setting, one's choice of office space may be quite limited. Office size, layout, access to windows and natural light, and general decor often leave much to be desired. Aging floor tiles, industrial carpet that has seen better days, walls painted in a monochromatic shade... these are not the atmospheric conditions that set souls free.

Add to that the periodic upheaval in having one's office location moved from one floor to another or one building to another as the powers that be decide to reconfigure space without your input, and you realize why control over your own office space can be a source of major satisfaction for the self-employed.

It is a good idea to visit other private practitioners or private rehabilitation companies to get a sense of what is practically and aesthetically appealing to you, what it all costs, and how you might plan your transition. A personal word about set and setting options: I have an office outside my home where I see patients, and an office in my home with a business line and fax machine, where I manage all other aspects of the practice (see Chapter 7). Some people prefer this situation for getting started, while others would rather make arrangement to work away from home, e.g., sublease an office one or two days a week from someone already well established in practice.

DEVELOPING YOUR OWN LETTERHEAD AND BROCHURES

You get to choose your own font, your own logo, and the color of your ink and stationery. You may print forms on your computer or order them from a printer. You can develop cards, letterhead, envelopes, notepads with your own distinctive layout, and carry that style over into the signage for your office door.

You can also develop your own marketing letters and brochures that describe your services, fees, hours, and location (see Chapter 6).

PERSONALIZED REPORT FORMATS

Mass-produced layouts of institutional transcription, even with well-typed reports, are not always user-friendly and readable. Although you may have control over the headings and format, you don't have control over the layout, spacing, paper quality, or font. These items are easy to negotiate with your own transcriptionist, on your own letterhead, and can add to the ease and readability of reports.

TEST SELECTION

I am sure this varies significantly from institution to institution, but occasionally, when new tests come out, or when one would like to have a particular set of software for scoring or testing, if this request was not submitted as part of the prior year's budget request, it can't be funded in an institutional setting until the following year. The request has to go through a process of form submission, approval, purchase order and so on, which adds a series of potentially unproductive, aggravating details to your day.

You do not have that problem in private practice. You pick up the phone, dial the 1-800 number for the test company, give your credit card number, and the materials are quickly on their way to you. Although you are buying these items with your own earnings, you can deduct their cost as a business expense and sometimes easily negotiate a shared or split cost with other colleagues in private practice.

TAX ADVANTAGES

The tax advantages in a private practitioner model surprised me, coming from many years in an institution-based practice. Everything spent for the business is deductible when you are self-employed (see Chapter 7 for more details).

EXERCISE: WHAT APPEALS MOST TO ME ABOUT PRIVATE PRACTICE?

1. List what you believe will be the top three or four advantages to you of private practice:

- *a. Significantly higher salary*
- *b. Control over total number of patients seen*
- *c. Control over which days of week you work*
- *d. First choice of vacation days*
- *e. More time with family and friends*
- *f. More time to travel or pursue other interests (e.g., music, art, sports)*
- *g. Other (fill in your own top preferences)*

2. Sketch out what you would consider an ideal daily, weekly, monthly, and annual schedule:

- *a. How many neuropsychological evaluations do you want to do each week?*
- *b. What will your working hours be each day?*
- *c. How much time do you want to save for teaching, research, or workshop development and delivery? Will these be paid work?*
- *d. Do you want to do legal work? If so, what percentage of your caseload?*
- *e. What conferences would you typically like to attend (e.g., International Neuropsychological Society (INS) in February, National Academy of Neuropsychology (NAN)in October, American Psychological Association (APA) in August.*
- *f. If you were to work part-time for a facility and part-time in your practice, which local facilities appeal to you?*

4

GETTING STARTED: PRACTICAL PRELIMINARY QUESTIONS

ARE YOU EXPERIENCED ENOUGH TO BE ON YOUR OWN?

Lack of business experience can be fairly quickly remedied with adequate planning, in-depth discussions with more experienced colleagues, and by gaining familiarity with your city and state's legal requirements. I think the more important question you must confront when you are planning to practice independently is your own level of clinical competence and experience in neuropsychology.

In general, I tend to discourage newly licensed psychologists in any subspecialty from immediately establishing their own private practice. Practicing alone with little independent experience is potentially problematic. Of course, there are certainly exceptions to this general rule. Sometimes there may be no other options besides self-employment, because of locale or circumstance. As you consider self-employment as a neuropsychologist, the following factors should be considered as honestly and clearly as possible:

1. How many years of experience have you accumulated in your training and in your postlicensure activities that are *directly* related to neuropsychology? Five years is a reasonable minimum.

2. If you are not board-certified, do you qualify to take the certification examination, based upon your education, training, and experience?
3. What is the range of patient populations with which you have worked?
4. What are your areas of special expertise (e.g., traumatic brain injury, the dementias, multiple sclerosis)?
5. Do you know when to refer to another practitioner?
6. Are you familiar with the ethical principles for your profession as a whole and for the ethical dilemmas that tend to arise in a neuropsychological practice?
7. How and where will you obtain ongoing consultation or supervision? This kind of resource can be critical to ensure that you are providing a consistently appropriate workup of your various patients, with a high quality report and effective follow-up with both your referral source and patient.

Even for experienced practitioners, quality of practice is likely to be improved by consultation. Consultation does not have to be limited to nearby colleagues, since colleagues you respect who live in other cities or states may be available to you. Although I think all of us should seek out colleagues with whom we can check our findings and opinions or share ideas, this kind of contact is particularly critical when one is a newly licensed psychologist or when one is beginning to work with a new and unfamiliar group of patients.

INDIVIDUAL OR GROUP PRACTICE

My private practice has always been an individual private practice. It was established after I had been in institution-based clinical work for 12 years. Because I wanted maximum control over all aspects of my work, and didn't want to negotiate on office space, personnel, fees, referral development, and other policies or choices, this made the most sense for me. I also wanted to be able to choose my own medical transcriptionist, who was familiar with neuropsychological and neurological terminology, and who shared my exacting standards for error-free reports.

One of the major challenges in beginning a solo private practice is that while your business is being built, you may not have a significant income. Setting aside enough money for start-up costs and a livable wage for at least 6 months reduces your financial stress. The support of a spouse or partner is also helpful.

Lack of initial cash flow may require that you do all of your own scheduling, phone calling, typing, copying, mailing, errand running for supplies and postage, billing, collections, banking, and tax preparation. Even some well-established solo practitioners continue to perform many of these basic functions as a way to keep overhead low. You will need to develop your own letterhead, business cards, marketing ideas, and determine ways to cover for vacations, sick days, and emergencies. You also need your own malpractice coverage and a business license, in addition to your psychology license.

For all of these reasons, some private practitioners prefer to start within the security of an established group practice, in which many of the above necessities are provided to you as a full member the group. Alternatively, you may establish your own individual practice in a group setting, where they share some but not all overhead costs, e.g., office space, parking, waiting room magazines and coffee, but not secretarial support.

At other times, you may have the option to become a partner or employee of an incorporated private practice group. Although there are excellent group practices or partnerships, it behooves you to be extremely careful before agreeing to participate in such a practice. Read the fine print, learn what expenses you are responsible for and learn if you have any control over shared expenses. Have an attorney review the contract, and look carefully at the procedures and requirements for exiting the agreement.

For example, in some group practices set up as corporations, the senior member may have considerable travel expenses that are considered part of the overhead that everyone must support, even though you may not be traveling much in your first year or two. Or there may be a clause in the contract that prevents you from setting up your own practice in the same city, if you decide to leave the group. You want to avoid being forced to commute from your community to a distant location where you are free to work because things didn't work out in the group practice.

Finally, it is a very good idea to obtain feedback from neuropsychologists, psychologists, physicians, nurses, or vocational counselors who have done business with the group practice or potential partner, to find out how satisfied they were with the group's service. If you are new in town and don't know the potential partners well, it is probably a good idea to check with your state psychology board and determine if there have been any complaints filed against any of them.

INTERDISCIPLINARY PRACTICES

It has been my experience that private practice opportunities for true interdisciplinary teamwork—as contrasted with multidisciplinary—are difficult to find in a free-standing, self-employment model. I am referring in particular to a combined neuropsychology and rehabilitation practice where both evaluations and subsequent treatment can be provided in a cohesive interdisciplinary fashion on site. In this model, treating professionals (including neuropsychology, clinical psychology, occupational therapy, physical therapy, speech, and vocational services, with medical consultation support), share space, time and daily contact, and they decide as a team upon the patients' major treatment themes and priorities. However, I have not seen this kind of private practice survive outside of a formal institutional or company setting.

However, while such a neurorehabilitation team is relatively rare in a freestanding independent group practice, it is entirely possible to form interesting groups of specialists. One such natural and compatible grouping may include a neuropsychologist, clinical psychologist, psychiatrist, and speech pathologist. Referrals may enter this group through any of those four specialties and are likely in many instances to result in further referrals to members of the group. For example, a patient referred for speech treatment may also need psychotherapy, medication consultation, and to have both abilities and difficulties documented by a neuropsychological evaluation.

You may know psychiatrists, physical therapists, and occupational therapists interested in a wide range of outpatient rehabilitation problems, including work hardening for pain patients, who may wish to have a compatible private practice group upon whom they can call for assistance with the cognitive, emotional, characterologic, neurobehavioral, and communication needs of their neurologically impaired patients.

Thus two smaller groups of practitioners may create formal or informal ties with one another to serve the best interest of their patients. This also benefits their practices. These groups can arrange to meet the patients at a particular site for team and family meetings and to promote well-integrated care in a noninstitutional setting.

FULL-TIME OR PART-TIME PRIVATE PRACTICE

For me, one of the most valuable aspects of private practice is that I can work far more satisfactorily than in most institutional settings, and can generate the same income in half the time. Although I was reasonably well paid during my institution-based years of employment, I typically worked a 50–60-hour week. I found that I could generate the same income—including the extra 23% needed to cover benefits—in approximately half that time.

In my own case, this included 12 guaranteed hours a week as a contract neuropsychologist for a private clinic, and about 12–15 hours a week at the higher rates of my own evaluation and consultation practices. I enjoyed 3 days off each week. This arrangement freed time to write, teach, and travel. More, I was able to pursue outcome research for which I previously had very little time and even less energy, when I was in 50–60-hour per week institutional employment.

For me, a part-time practice is satisfying. I also have the flexibility to increase the hours if I know I am going to be away for several weeks and wish to generate extra income to help carry me through that time.

Even in a full-time private practice, most of my colleagues try to arrange their clinical work 4 days per week. You might reserve this 5th day for paperwork, a few hours of billing and calls, for time with family, for a 3-day vacation. Arrangements can also be made to sublet space and equipment during this day out of the office, so another person getting started part-time can pay to use your office and testing materials (see Chapter 7 for other suggestions.)

CONSULTATION OR SUPERVISION PRACTICES

You may decide that you do not wish to have a clinical practice; rather, you prefer to consult or supervise. This option is especially useful for experienced neuropsychologists who have established a good reputation and whose expertise is in demand.

There may be a variety of self-insured companies, private nurse case managers, younger psychologists wishing to accrue supervised hours towards licensure, or colleagues with the occasional thorny case, who would like to obtain your services now that you are available. After years of clinical work and development of professional expertise, it can be refreshing to find that you need not involve yourself further with the profound irritations of managed care, or trying to get on panels, or waiting for reimbursements to arrive from tardy insurance companies. It also doesn't require an act of God, working through an institutional billing office, to have some say in what is charged, what is allowed, and what will be collected. Instead, you will be directly and fully paid for your time. (Please note: if you are still dealing with managed care, see Chapters 5 and 7 for relevant pointers.)

TEACHING

There are often a number of interesting teaching options in your community. These may include classroom teaching, continuing education workshops, in-service instruction for rehabilitation companies, or creating and running your own continuing education course. I will review these one at time.

Classroom Teaching

Even if there are not formal part-time positions available to you, you may be able to offer your services as a locum teacher, covering for instructors on vacation or other leave. Check with the psychology departments in colleges and universities to see if they have a course that needs covering in the next year. Sometimes it is possible to cover for only a couple of lectures, but doing so can create future teaching opportunities.

Workshops

Your state psychology association or other professional organizations to which you belong may sponsor continuing education coursework for their members. This might be a 3-hour course that you teach, independent of annual conferences, for which you will be paid around $250.

In-Service Training

Rehabilitation companies for whom you may consult on a contract basis often have training needs for their staff. In addition to whatever neuropsychology work you provide, you may also be able to develop and deliver staff training modules.

Developing and Running Your Own Continuing Education Course

Some of my colleagues have successfully organized 1- or 2-day courses on topics of interest in the neuropsychology, rehabilitation, and legal communities. For example, a forum on mild traumatic brain injury and persisting postconcussion syndrome may be of broad interest to your colleagues in many related fields of service.

MEDICAL-LEGAL WORK

What I call “medical-legal work may involve the following (See Chapter 8 for further comments):

1. Conducting a neuropsychological evaluation as part of an independent medical evaluation (IME). These are often requested by state worker compensation systems or by self-insured companies who have an injured worker.
2. Evaluating a patient as part of a personal injury case, with the request originating from either the plaintiff or defense attorney, as part of their gathering of relevant information prior to trial or mediation.
3. Testifying about a past clinical evaluation that is now being called into evidence as part of a legal case;
4. Conducting a neuropsychological evaluation as requested by a guardian ad litem, who has been appointed to protect the interests and safety of an elderly person, or someone for whom there are mental competency concerns.

5. Reviewing records or prior neuropsychological evaluation reports and data in any of the above circumstances, to comment on what has been done, its appropriateness, and its limitations. You may also be asked to make recommendations for further workup or treatment of the client. In this latter instance, you may or may not be the person who eventually provides that further workup or treatment.

NEUROPSYCHOLOGICAL EVALUATIONS AND EXPERT WITNESS WORK

Whether you seek it or not, opportunities to be an expert witness are likely to come seeking you when you practice as a neuropsychologist. In two particular instances this is likely to be true: (a) patients with acquired TBI who were injured in motor vehicle accidents or at work and (b) competency issues for dementing patients. You may find yourself on the witness stand even though the patient referral came initially from a physician who was seeking to clarify clinical, treatment, or diagnostic concerns.

Medical-legal work can certainly be lucrative, especially in contrast to some managed care reimbursement. I know psychologists whose entire practices are forensic. I also know psychologists who make it clear from the outset that they do not want to do legal work, and that if called as witnesses, they are going to be unhappy witnesses.

My own position and the one I generally recommend to people establishing a practice lies closer to the "do not seek it, and it will find you" end of the spectrum. Trying to function as an expert witness when you are not yet an expert is probably not a good idea. It is, however, reasonable to begin with a case that you know well, if you have the choice in an area of your strongest experience, such as severe TBI. As part of my initial interview, I have learned to always inquire if there is a pending legal case, or if there is an attorney involved. This fact can affect some aspects of test selection, such as measures of effort and/or premorbid IQ estimates that you might not otherwise use routinely.

On the one hand, I think too much legal work can be limiting to the range of patients you see, and therefore limiting to your general level of neuropsychological expertise. On the other hand, I think having your opinions and procedures challenged can be a good way to reexamine them.

As a side note, it is also an interesting way to see what other neuropsychologists are using as part of their full workups or how they format their reports. There are, however, probably easier ways to determine this than taking on a legal case.

Finally, there is always the satisfaction that can come with a job well done, or feeling that your opinion helped in some way to obtain a fair resolution. If this becomes your primary motivation for taking on this work, however, you run the risk of evolving into an arm-waving advocate or a cynical naysayer, rather than a scientist-practitioner whose priority is to present the truth as clearly as possible.

About 5% of my practice in any given year is medical-legal work resulting from a direct attorney referral. An additional 5% of my clinical patients eventually bring with them some discussion with attorneys or depositions and, rarely, a court appearance. At this time I conduct three or four evaluations a week, 46 weeks a year, for about 170 patients a year. So, about two patients in any given month are likely to have medical legal issues. Average fees per case typically include an extensive record review, a full evaluation and report, and consultations with the attorney. You can estimate, based upon your hourly rates, the kind of revenue this would generate for you.

HOSPITAL AND CLINIC AFFILIATIONS

There are features of an institution-based practice that strengthen or augment a private practice, and vice versa, in a way that is hard to achieve solely within one domain. When leaving institutional practice, or when considering whether to join an institution-based practice, try not to take the all-or-none approach. A cornerstone of the scientist-practitioner model is to take the best of both forms of employment and combine them to suit your needs.

One way to do that in a hospital setting is to provide part-time psychology and neuropsychology services on an inpatient rehabilitation unit, on the acute floors for patients with neurologic problems, or in a skilled nursing facility. You may be hired as a regular part-time employee, with benefits, or as a contract or hourly employee of the facility. In either circumstance negotiate that the facility pays for your malpractice insurance to cover your work with its patients. The institution should also be responsible for scheduling, billing, and providing dictation support.

In those settings, you may be asked to conduct brief screening evaluations or consult with staff about behavioral management issues. You may also speak with families about cognitive and personality changes to expect after neurologic injuries or with dementia, or about outpatient neurorehabilitation treatments available after discharge.

In a private outpatient clinic, you may join a particular department, such as primary care, neurology, or behavioral health and provide their neuropsychological services, with the same understanding about scheduling, secretarial support for phones, liability insurance, dictation, billing, and collections. In return, you will agree to accept a much lower rate of pay (e.g., $45–50 per hour) than you might be able to collect on your own, if they will guarantee a certain minimum number of hours per week and cover your overhead and practice costs.

UNIVERSITY OR MEDICAL SCHOOL POSITIONS

Many universities and medical schools have part-time clinical faculty positions. These positions typically involve direct patient care, supervision of graduate students, interns, or postdoctoral fellows, and teaching. The combination will depend upon a variety of factors.

In a college or university psychology department, for example, someone may be needed to provide care in a student health service or in a psychology outpatient clinic where community patients are treated. You would likely be providing supervision to advanced graduate students or residents. If you are trained and interested in providing psychotherapy as well as neuropsychological services, this may be a good entry point for you.

In a medical school setting, the various departments (e.g., rehabilitation medicine, psychiatry and behavioral sciences, neurology, neurosurgery, a regional epilepsy center, and all these departments in a children's hospital and medical center) are likely to have clinical faculty positions. These may be hourly or salaried positions, depending upon the institution.

In some instances, if these clinical faculty positions are at the .5 full-time equivalent (FTE) level, there will be noncompete clauses with which to contend. That is, you are not allowed to have a private practice. However, if you can demonstrate that you will do only evaluations (or only treatment) in one setting and not in the other, you may be able to negotiate an exception to this policy.

A colleague of mine was recently able to negotiate such an arrangement. She conducts a well-established private practice, and spends about half her time in evaluation work and half her time providing psychotherapy. The agreement is that she will transfer her neuropsychological evaluation practice to a private medical center. She will provide neuropsychological evaluations and some occasional inpatient coverage only at the center, work half time there, and receive all pertinent benefits and privileges, including health insurance and retirement benefits.

In return, she agrees to see only psychotherapy patients in her private practice, which is a long and well-established practice in the community. She was not required to sign a noncompete clause, as her practice far predated the institutional job offer. If for any reason things don't work out well with the medical center, she has the immediate option to return full-time to her private practice. While she would not take the clinic patients with her, she can certainly take her long-standing referral sources for neuropsychological evaluations or treatment with her.

ADJUNCT APPOINTMENTS

In this kind of arrangement, you may arrange to teach a class for either undergraduates or graduate psychology students. The institution may have a course or two that cannot currently be covered by their regular faculty. Depending on the institution, you may be paid about $3,000 for teaching one class.

In addition to bringing clinical experience to the department's courses and to the students' education, your colleagues have an opportunity to observe you work, conceptualize issues, and interact. This may lead to a more permanent teaching position. This opportunity can also function indirectly as a form of marketing and may plant the seed for later referrals to your practice, even though that is not the primary intention of your teaching.

I hope it also goes without saying that you should not be recruiting students as patients, subjects or as personal friends. If they need psychology services, you would guide them to an appropriate referral.

In a medical school, you may provide clinical supervision for neuropsychology or rehabilitation postdoctoral fellows, meeting with them on a weekly or biweekly basis to discuss cases. This supervision will function as a form of continuing education for you as well as for these students. They will benefit from your clinical experiences, and you will benefit from their up-to-date knowledge of the literature as well as their enthusiasm and thought-provoking questions. Such adjunct appointments also typically bring a variety of faculty privileges, such as access to library and catalog information, article reprint services, and access to the Internet.

PART-TIME CLINICAL FACULTY

Within a medical school setting, there may be clinical faculty positions available, on a half-time or less basis, to assist with evaluation and treatment services. Psychologists in these positions are not required to publish. Some teaching, supervision, and plenty of clinical work usually comprise the key responsibilities.

Neuropsychologists in particular can be in an enviable position with respect to noncompete clauses usually associated with half-time or greater positions in medical school settings. Noncompete clauses typically include two components:

1. If you work for the institution at a half-time or greater level, so that you receive health, vacation and retirement benefits, you may not conduct a practice anywhere else.
2. If you decide to terminate, you may not establish a practice within a 50-mile radius of the institution where you worked.

There are some important exceptions made to these basic rules, which are especially applicable to neuropsychologists. First, we do not constitute a significant practice threat to a medical school, as we are not going to join them for 2 years and then take a substantial money-making operation (e.g., their lung transplant program) to a nearby competing hospital. The amount of money involved in the typical neuropsychology practice does not loom large within a medical school or hospital setting.

Second, if you are coming to the institution from a well-established practice of your own, you have the right to return to that practice with no penalty if you ever leave the institution. You would have presumably brought your patients and referral sources to the institution when you arrived and would have the right to reestablish yourself locally with those same resources. These are important points in any negotiation with an institution, and you should not be persuaded to sign a noncompete clause or loyalty oath under these circumstances.

One further negotiating point for neuropsychologists considering a part-time clinical faculty appointment is to differentiate an evaluation practice from a psychotherapy or treatment practice. For example, you may negotiate a half-time position (which usually brings full benefits) within a medical school to do only certain kinds of evaluation, screening, or group treatment of brain-injured patients there. You may still maintain a private practice outside the institution that is solely a psychotherapy treatment practice or a more focused evaluation practice for diagnostic groups you would never encounter in the institution. Many institutions allow an outside medical-legal practice, for non-institution patients, conducted on your own time.

Finally, in a university or medical school setting, there may be co-principal investigator grant opportunities, or subprojects within a grant, where your position is paid directly from the grant. These grants are typically funded for 3–5-year periods, so you can depend upon the income. There is incentive to stay current on the relevant literature, which can result in shared authorship on publications if you are interested. It also may provide (a) financial support for attending professional meetings and (b) ongoing involvement with academic colleagues.

In these ways you can develop guaranteed sources of income that also offset the potential isolation and reduced intellectual stimulation of a solo private practice. As you can see there are many interesting and creative ways to craft a practice that pays well and consistently, and allows clinical, teaching, supervision, and research time in some appealing combination, along with a good degree of freedom.

EXERCISE: HOW TO EXPLORE AND DEFINE YOUR OPTIONS

1. *What are my practice options in the place I would like to live?*
   a. *Is there a niche for me in the current private practice market? Are there underserved populations of patients or parts of town that do not have a good neuropsychologist?*

b. *How many colleges or universities would have part-time teaching work? Whom do I call to determine this?*
c. *Which institutions might be interested in a contract psychologist to provide neuropsychological services? Rehabilitation services? Other clinical services?*
d. *Which groups of physicians or other health care practitioners might be open to sharing office space and referrals with a neuropsychologist? Are there good local neurologists or physiatrists in private practice?*

2. *Can I create a reasonable source of income from a combination of these settings, employers, and options?*

5

A PRACTICAL GUIDE FOR OPENING YOUR BUSINESS

DON'T BURN BRIDGES

Although "don't burn bridges" is generally good advice for living, it is particularly important as you launch into your own business, where both your reputation, and the integrity of your professional relationships are likely to make a significant difference to the success of your practice, happiness, and peace of mind. Don't destroy, weaken, sully, or abandon prior working relationships because you think you have no further interest or use for those past connections.

When you develop your plans for leaving an institution, give your employer plenty of advance notice so your replacement can be recruited. Don't take business from your prior place of employment, and do what you can to smooth the transition of the new employee, if that is at all feasible. You never know what the future may hold. Although you cannot imagine it now, you may want to return one day to this institution. Or you may simply want to cooperate with the institution in the care of given patients.

Further, do not disparage other practitioners of your art and science, regardless of their affiliation. This may seem obvious, but it may be a particularly tempting impulse when you are called as an expert witness and discover that a neuropsychologist on the other side has written an inflammatory opinion in response to your findings and report. Do not allow yourself to be pulled into the silly or intemperate behavior that seems to be the delight of some forensic and legal practitioners. Try to remember that an expert witness is a neutral witness; you are there to accurately present and interpret the data to the best of your ability. Competent people can disagree on their interpretation; you don't need to destroy someone else's reputation to prove your own point. Politely disagree, make your points as effectively as possible, and move on.

CLINICIAN, KNOW THYSELF

If you are going to practice on your own, you need to have accurate knowledge of your personal and professional strengths and weaknesses. Know which kinds of patients you feel comfortable seeing, which kinds of patients you do not or should not see, and have a clear idea of how you will screen and triage patients.

You also need to know your own work habits. Are you well organized? When your day is not structured by an institution, are you disciplined enough to stick with an internally imposed schedule? Do you have the patience to deal with managed care companies or the resources to hire some preauthorization, billing, and collections support for this part of your practice?

Are you able to market your practice effectively and stick with a marketing plan, even if you are naturally somewhat shy or procrastinating? Are you averse to direct solicitation of business? If so, do you have a set of alternatives in mind? Are you willing to seek out and if necessary pay other practitioners for some advice? Do you feel comfortable calling primary care providers in your area and visiting their departments to provide information about your services?

Are you able to negotiate fees? Do you feel comfortable requiring a deposit for your services? Will you assist with pursuit of collecting them?

All of the above, and more, are likely to be necessary to run a successful independent practice.

A MOVEABLE FEAST: THE MENU OF PRACTICE OPTIONS

As mentioned in Chapter 4, many practice options are available to you. For most people getting started in self-employment, it helps to have some kind of income you can count on every month, as well as more variable income from referrals or activities that will grow as your practice evolves. Below are several additional ways to get started by including contractual work.

MAINTAIN A PART-TIME PRACTICE WITH YOUR PREVIOUS EMPLOYER

A number of colleagues I know have continued employment on a part-time basis with their previous employers while establishing a private practice in a somewhat different domain of evaluation or treatment. For example, they continue to see patients for treatment at a hospital or clinic, but do only neuropsychological evaluations in their private practice (or vice versa).

DEVELOPING A SAFETY NET: STARTING WITH A GROUP

Perhaps you would like to leave your institution. One safe way is to identify a well-established group private practice in your community. In some group practices, the owners of the practice will be willing to guarantee a base number of referrals per month. This latter course may be especially likely if the group practice is well established or their neuropsychologist has recently moved elsewhere, and the practice members want you to enter their busy group and take over this part of the practice. Or they may be willing initially to charge flat rental rates, on the days you want to use office space and testing equipment, with the understanding that you will bring your own referrals. In this circumstance, you are not responsible for paying overhead unless you have income.

In either situation, one of the advantages of an established group practice is that testing equipment and space are usually available, so you can avoid an initial outlay of several thousand dollars to purchase testing materials. You also don't need to pay monthly office rent when you don't yet have income. Once your business is thriving, these fees may be negotiable, and in fact, that issue should be part of your initial discussion: At what point would it be worth it for you to pay a monthly rate for the space, rather than x amount per day or hours of use?

OFFERING CONTRACT SERVICES TO INPATIENT REHABILITATION UNITS

One of the many positive factors that accrues from maintaining ties with inpatient rehabilitation units is that you can help create or preserve a neuropsychology presence in an environment that is all too often unaware of this resource. You can teach colleagues how to make most effective use of it. You might negotiate for quarter-time salaried employee position or for a contractual relationship. The latter option may be worth your while if the hospital covers your malpractice insurance in that setting, supports your equipment needs, does your billing and collections, and pays you an hourly rate.

You should expect to see the patients on your roster, attend pertinent team meetings, do your dictation, and be free to leave. You should also make arrangements to have psychiatric emergencies covered by the in-house team of physicians, who can arrange for medications or mental health admissions in a way that you cannot.

Usually by working less than half time, you avoid noncompete clauses and yet keep some interesting patients, physicians, and team contacts in your schedule. You can also be available as a resource for subsequent outpatient referrals as part of your private practice, if they do not have an on-site practitioner who provides these services.

OFFERING CONTRACT SERVICES TO PRIVATE CLINICS

You may wish to choose a specialty department, or a primary care department, or a mental health department, within a private clinic with satellite branches, and approach the department chair about providing neuropsychological evaluation or consultation on a contractual basis. I usually offer to present a good teaching case, which can clearly demonstrate to the department members that a good evaluation, report, and follow-up with family and the patient can greatly facilitate the patient's improved function, and augment the effectiveness of the physicians' care.

The evaluation should be presented, with the patient's identity protected, at one of the department's weekly case conferences. The department members will get to know you better; they usually have a good understanding of the particular diagnostic issue, what the medical problems are, and can see the practical relevance of what you do. Forming these kinds of relationships with a particular department, in a clinic that does not routinely offer neuropsychological services, should be done with an eye to the kinds of patients you want to see (e.g., tumor patients, multiple sclerosis patients, differential diagnosis patients, dementia patients) that you may not routinely see in your own office. It is also a good way to demonstrate the benefits of integrated patient care (i.e., how it helps to have a specialty care provider like you as part of the medical team).

Further, these same clinicians may also approach you in your private practice for clinical assistance with their friends who need neuropsychological services. They may send members of their family to see you, outside their own clinic, for reasons of confidentiality.

MEMBERSHIP IN MANAGED CASE PANELS

In order to bill some insurance companies, you need to be a member of their list of approved providers, i.e., on their panel of providers. In some instances, as a new, independent private practitioner, it is truly impossible to get on panels when they are closed to new members. This is one further reason that starting your private practice with institution based, part-time employment can be helpful. Institutions usually have well-established contracts with a plethora of managed health companies, since large institutions see such a wide variety of patients.

Once you are listed as a provider on an insurance health plan through an institution, it is often a relatively easy matter to simply add your private practice address and tax ID number where you will continue to see patients covered by this same insurance company. I explained to a number of third party payment organizations that I was not asking them to add me as a new provider, since I already had been seeing their patients, but to simply expand or change the locations where I would see their patients. Once you have been seeing these patients, it is my understanding that you cannot be refused permission to continue to see them, even if you now work for a different local employer (i.e., yourself).

You should also contact both your state worker compensation board and your state division of vocational rehabilitation to become an official provider. You should be able to obtain a provider number. You can also ask about their rates of reimbursement and rules for billing, and so on.

You may also wish to contact the local Social Security Disability agency. They are often looking to hire psychologists and neuropsychologists to do basic disability testing and screening. In addition, they are interested in hiring experienced psychologists for case review, which simply involves reviewing records and making recommendations on the basis of the testing that has already been done.

I decided not to be either a Medicare or Medicaid provider in my private practice. I wanted to reduce the amount of bureaucracy in my life, not increase it. I also find the ever increasing number of government regulations to be a source of added time and expense, with no clear benefit to me or my patients. A number of my neuropsychology colleagues in private practice have told me that they find dealing with Medicare to be fairly reasonable, and reimbursement rates, especially with a secondary insurance, are adequate for both evaluation and treatment. Medicaid continues to pay very little for psychology services of any kind.

OBTAINING ADJUNCT OR CLINICAL TEACHING APPOINTMENTS

As previously mentioned, I encourage you to establish ties with universities or medical schools as an adjunct or clinical faculty. The affiliation usually brings with it an opportunity to teach, to provide clinical supervision for graduate students, psychology interns, or postdoctoral fellows; to collaborate on writing or research projects; and to access library resources. It may also strengthen your credibility with the private practice community if you are new to town and otherwise unknown.

While it always helps to know someone in the department, it is also effective to send a curriculum vitae and letter of interest to a psychology department chair, outlining the areas where you might be able to be of direct service. In a medical school setting, you may wish to send the letter and curriculum vitae to the chief psychologist in the department, then follow up from there with a call to see if an appointment time can be made.

It is also helpful to identify the faculty in advance and look up their work via the Internet, as well as research basic information on the academic institution. While it is certainly useful to know the department's training needs, their philosophy of treatment, and how your skills and interests may supplement, newcomers to a city are not expected to know everything about a particular setting. That is part of the reason for having a discussion to determine if your interests, aptitudes, and needs fit well with the institution's needs.

HOW TO DETERMINE FAIR FEES

When I was starting in private practice in 1993, I looked at the range of fees being charged throughout my community (Seattle) in both institutional and private settings, and I selected the median. At that time, the median fee was $125 an hour; over time, I gradually increased my clinical fees to $150 an hour. The 2003 hourly rates here range from approximately $116 to $170 an hour, with a standard evaluation requiring 12 hrs. This time includes all record review, interview, testing administration and scoring, review of results, and dictation of a report. It does not typically include the feedback session, which is charged separately.

Some well-established practitioners in private practice simply charge a flat fee for delivering an evaluation, usually in the $2,000–$2,200 range. I have seen some evaluations done for as much as $3,000 in legal cases, and some for as little as $740 (for a fixed menu of tests with vocational rehabilitation clients).

For legal work, I followed the guidelines of the institution where I originally practiced:

1. Clinical exams and record review are charged at your regular clinical rate.
2. All consultation time with attorneys, whether by phone or in person, is billed at $400 an hour.

3. Any deposition time held at your convenience in the office of your choice, is billed at $400 an hour, with a 2-hour minimum.

4. All courtroom appearances in the city are charged at $400 an hour, with a minimum of 4 hours. By the time you drive to the courthouse, park, wait for the elevators, find the courtroom, wait your turn, testify, and reverse all those steps to get back to the office, you will probably have spent most or all of a morning or afternoon. And you have lost the chance to do a neuropsychological evaluation that day. You need to be reimbursed for your lost business, and for the stress often associated with testimony. If the courthouse is at some distance, I negotiate with the attorney to hire a car and driver to take me to and from the courthouse, maximizing the efficiency of my time. I can review records, return phone calls, or read journals during the commute.

HOW TO FIND GOOD HELP

If you are new to town, immediately join the local neuropsychological society. Look up the psychologists and neuropsychologists, in both institutional settings and in private practice, introduce yourself, and invite them to lunch. At lunch, ask them for advice. For example, how did they find good psychometrists, transcriptionists, office help, accountants, and preauthorization and billing help? What do they think are some unmet neuropsychology needs in the community?

At many institutions, psychometrists and secretaries may be employed on a part-time or contractual basis, are well experienced, and would be happy to have additional self-employment income. Even if they are not interested, they may have friends and colleagues to recommend. It has been my experience that the neuropsychology and rehabilitation communities for brain-impaired patients are really quite small, even in a large city. It is in everyone's best interest to know each other and to know where to find experienced help of all kinds, for patients and their testing and treatment needs.

It is also very helpful to speak with the local speech pathology community. Speech pathologists in private practice have many of the same professional issues and concerns as self-employed neuropsychologists. These include preauthorization of evaluation and treatment services for neurologically impaired patients, dictation of reports, proper submission of billing codes and tax help from accountants who understand this kind of business. In addition, the speech pathology community often has strong ties with physicians, and they may be open to the benefits of a mutually cooperative practice relationship with neuropsychology.

DEVELOPING A BUSINESS PLAN AND PRACTICE MANAGEMENT STATISTICS

A good business plan includes the development of concrete facts and numbers. These include the amount of your fixed monthly expenses. That is, those items that are absolute in cost and must be paid each month no matter what, such as office rent and monies owed to your transcriptionist and phone service. It helps to think of the bills you will be receiving each month, including utilities, tests ordered, and postage. Check with colleagues about their fixed expense categories or with a good accountant who understands a psychology private practice.

The plan should also include a realistic assessment of how much money you need to earn so that you net enough on a weekly or monthly basis to be paid a reasonable salary after your fixed expenses are met. Although many practitioners begin merely trying to meet basic expenses, hoping to develop an improving salary, you need to have a good sense of how much work you need to schedule in order to make self-employment a realistic enterprise on a long-term basis.

Having 6 months of expense funds in reserve is a minimum nest egg with which to get started. This insures you can remain open for business even if you have no income for six months. When you have calculated your basic monthly expense estimates, it is prudent to add another 30% to those figures, just to be on the safe side.

When you are calculating what you are likely to collect each month, it is a good idea initially to deduct 30% from those estimates, to be on the safe side. Sometimes, an evaluation bill that you fully expected to be paid immediately may undergo strange migrations within the insurance payment system and may have to be resubmitted for reasons that are not your fault. All it takes is one of those in a given month to reduce your income by $1,000.

Your business plan also needs to include a system for collecting monthly statistics for the various services you perform. It will be important to have cold, hard facts: what you charge, what portion of those charges you receive, and what your monthly income actually is.

This monthly tracking system could be set up as part of your referral log, but it should include, at a minimum, information about who referred the patient, the diagnosis, services you provided, the total hours billed within each category (e.g., 96117, 96115, or one of the health and behavior codes), which insurance company was supposed to pay the bill or a portion of it, amount of deposit you initially collected from the patient, how soon you submitted your billing after the service was provided, and how long it took to receive payment.

You will then begin to understand what the referral and reimbursement parameters of your practice are becoming. In this way, you can better plan your revenue-generating activities. You may decide as a result of these emerging statistics to alter the way you practice. For example, you might change your patient mix; or you might cultivate additional referrals from sources who you have learned pay quickly and fairly; you may decide to increase the deposit that must come from patients with certain kinds of poor insurance coverage; or to take on guaranteed contract work while your practice is still building.

When you discover what it takes to live and thrive professionally, you can focus upon particular markets of patients and referral sources to further sustain your practice. These data you are collecting will also guide you through other business decisions. For instance, you may one day decide you should hire a part-time billing and collections person and pay them a percentage of what is collected in order to create time for yourself to generate more billable hours of clinical work.

You need to remain open to the possibility, even the likelihood, that you will revise your original business plan in order to conform to your growing understanding of market realities. Perhaps the neuropsychology market is saturated in your city with people performing evaluations. It may be, however, that not enough people provide treatment to these patients. Or, perhaps there are geographic areas of saturation, which you can avoid by leasing part-time office space a few miles distant from your original location. You may discover a relatively underserved area, and physician providers will welcome you to the neighborhood, with referrals soon coming your way.

When you collect and monitor information about your revenue and expenses, weekly schedule, and clinical cachement area, you maximize your opportunities for changing some of those realities to support the success of your practice. When you know what is missing, or which activity is unproductive, you are then able to confront the problem. You might make relatively quick changes, in some instances, or put plans in place that will begin to pay off in the relatively short term.

For example, although I enjoyed teaching psychology courses at a small private university in the early days of my private practice, it took substantial time to prepare lectures, commute to campus, deliver the lectures, meet with students, score tests, and read and score term papers. When I divided my salary by the actual hours I spent I found I was earning $8 an hour. I couldn't afford to teach these courses and I needed to find other outlets for the pleasure that teaching provided. I began to teach workshops and offered lectures that became marketing tools for my practice. I still miss teaching undergraduate college courses, but in order to make self-employment viable—and not go back to the 60-hour week I had happily left behind in my full-time institutional days,—it was a necessary shift in emphasis.

EXERCISE: TIMELINE FOR IMPLEMENTING YOUR PRACTICE TEMPLATE

You have now decided what combination of activities you want in your practice. Make a list of those activities and roles or jobs.

How do you plan to transition from your current employment situation to take on these other responsibilities? Will you quit completely? Will you scale down to part-time? Do you plan to secure part-time employment someplace else prior to leaving your current job?

Will you be joining a group or other well-established private practice, and are they willing to provide some of the start-up support costs, expecting repayment once you are established?

Have you saved enough money to live for 6 months without much salary? Do you have a spouse or partner willing to support you during this period of transition? If you need a loan you will feel more secure if you arrange it while you are still employed full time at your current job.

What rate of income growth, over the next 6 months to 2 years, will make private practice a viable option for you?

6

MARKETING AND OTHER MATTERS

FIRST AND FOREMOST, DO GOOD WORK

You may not realize that a fundamental tool for marketing your practice is simply doing good work. You might be surprised, though, to discover how hard it is to find neuropsychologists who are both clinically skilled and scientifically sound. Neuropsychologists are generally an intelligent group, and probably prefer a thorough if not somewhat obsessive craft. There is, however, a fine line between adequate understanding and effective performance. This is, in part, because what we know and understand about test measurement and brain function is yet incomplete. In addition, fine discriminations in a patient's test performance that are important to our analysis and synthesis may be difficult to communicate to the nonneuropsychologist. It is challenging at times to link our findings to specific interventions. Other practitioners sometimes rightly complain that we do not translate our findings into useful and practical implications or treatment recommendations for the patient.

Furthermore, I think neuropsychologists as a group, lovable as we may be when you get to know us well, sometimes don't have the interpersonal sensitivity for patients and colleagues that one might wish. Aside from the occasional lack of social grace and potential for data-based narcissism in some members, there are too often fixed and loudly defended positions on any of a number of questions that should remain open to discussion among the members of our craft. Is the American Board of Professional Psychology's diplomate a superior form of certification? Is National Academy of Neuropsychology a more responsive and clinically relevant organization than is International Neuropsychological Society? Does the quantitative versus process approach to assessment really divide experienced practitioners as absolutely as some insist? These are all questions that give the thinking neuropsychologist pause, and they are not unimportant or trivial questions.

But while we are debating the fine points of a particular approach, or using our reports as vehicles to defend a particular position or criticize someone else's, our referring providers and patients may be left to flounder in a morass of data without meaningful conclusions. My goal is to provide clinically useful reports, render scientifically sound conclusions, and offer practical recommendations for patients and their providers. It is a primary goal I recommend to you in your practice as well.

Practice within your scope of knowledge, and don't make any of the following mistakes: Don't pretend you know things that you don't. Don't pretend that everyone else in the business is ignorant. Don't routinely assume that people with mild brain injury are almost always subtlely brain damaged for life, or, alternatively, couldn't possibly have had any kind of permanent organic change that is relevant to real-life function. We need daily reminders to be respectful, open-minded in the context of a well-established and updated knowledge base, and to learn as much as we can about how people with particular neuropsychological patterns actually function in their lives.

If you are a neuropsychologist without much rehabilitation or individual psychotherapy experience, your ability to make meaningful connections with patients or co-workers may be more limited than you realize. You might be an exception. Consider, though, that lack of these particular formative experiences, and an adequate level of comfort with them, may also reduce your ability to develop meaningful and practical recommendations on the patients' and families' behalf. Or, you may have good ideas about compensatory techniques, but not be able to effectively and sympathetically provide feedback in a manner the patient can hear and accept.

If you are a neuropsychologist with a minimum of experience and training in brain anatomy, physiology, neurologic injuries, and disease processes, you may have good treatment recommendations, but you may be prone to other errors, such as misdiagnosing a concussion when the underlying problem is early Alzheimer's disease. Further, if you are not well grounded in assessment and no longer administer your own tests, you may be less able to make appropriate test selection and to assess qualitative test issues for particular patients.

The effective practitioner is a reasonable human being who can see shades of grey where others may only see black and white. She or he can also distinguish black from white and doesn't minimize one or the other because it (a) doesn't support a personal or strongly held expectation, (b) might hurt someone's feelings, or (c) will likely discourage a lucrative referral source. Those who want only to purchase a particular opinion or bias are not worth your time. If you try to serve them, you may find yourself an unwitting member of the world's oldest profession, rather than a scientist-practitioner.

We can't rise to every challenge all of the time, but some wisely selected challenges will help you establish a thriving and long-lasting private practice. For example, how to get the further training and experience that you need, as well as how to be both a good human being and a good neuropsychologist are worthy challenges. Of course, these aren't the only factors that matter—a certain amount of luck, love in your life, and a little money don't hurt, either.

THE INTRODUCTORY LETTER: BE SPECIFIC BUT NOT TOO LIMITING

When I receive marketing letters from psychologists, one of the first things I notice is that some are often not specific enough about the kinds of patients they want to see. Nor are these letters as forthcoming as I would like about the psychologist's background, experience with particular populations, and training. When I receive such a limited letter, I don't have sufficient information to lead me to make a referral.

When I know the kinds of patients someone wants to see, or what their particular areas of expertise or interest might be, I am more likely to contact the person. (See Appendix for two sample marketing letters, one generic, one more specific.)

I think it is also helpful for the marketing neuropsychologist to include a line or two in the letter, at the end, that says something like, "In the next few months, I hope to have the chance to speak with you about your practice, interests, and needs. Thank you for keeping me in mind when you make referrals for neuropsychology services. Please feel free to contact me if you have any questions about my practice."

Remember that as a self-employed practitioner, you are also necessarily in sales. Although that does not have to be your preeminent thought, it needs to occupy a space in your conscious awareness. With your marketing letter, you are at the very least trying to open a discussion with a potential referral source. Following-up with a meeting over coffee or lunch may allow you to "close the deal" with an initial referral.

DEVELOP SEMINARS AND WORKSHOPS

If you have a particular area of expertise, why not develop a local workshop on the topic and arrange for continuing education (CE) credits? For instance, a Thursday or Friday afternoon workshop for four hours of CE credit at $50 a person, for which you provide handouts, and refreshments may be a profitable marketing investment. If you only break even you are nonetheless setting the stage for good conversations with peers. And, there is nothing like the requirements of good teaching to help you hone your own skills, and take the time to keep current with the literature. And you are likely to have the kind of brainstorming and discussion that can lead to growth and increased knowledge on your part as well as for your audience.

You can develop these workshops on your own, or in cooperation with a local agency or group (such as the Multiple Sclerosis Society, the Alzheimer's Disease and Related Disorders organization or the Brain Injury Association). You can negotiate a fee for your talk, and, of course, you will have add increased your recognition as a knowledgeable and approachable neuropsychologist by this exposure to the community.

GIVE GUEST LECTURES

Academicians usually enjoy a break from regular classroom instruction. Offering guest lectures can stir the students' interest with actual clinical material or with a new topic (e.g., the neuropsychology of multiple sclerosis), and it's a great way to establish contact in the community. You will at least meet a faculty member with whom you might have coffee and perhaps more connections in the future. You also can connect with a group of fledgling psychologists or physicians who will know your name, phone number, and email address to use for future consultation or referral after their training is complete.

You never know from whence referrals or satisfying work relationships will spring. You are planting seeds—some will fall on fallow ground, but many will take hold in ways you couldn't have imagined at the time.

OFFER A MEMORY COURSE TO THE PUBLIC

Creating lecturers for the public is also a terrific way to make money, do good, have fun, and get your name out and about in the community of people who have memory concerns or who have relatives with neurologic disorders. You might arrange this to be a morning course, for an hour a week for 4 weeks. You might charge a fee of $40, and provide an attractive notebook of instructional materials, coffee, and cookies. With a minimum enrollment of 10 people, you may have already done the math; You stand to earn $400 for 4 hours of direct instruction and you are simultaneously becoming known to the public.

If fewer than ten people show up, you can decide if you should cancel the course, reschedule it, or hold it any way. Most of us have more time than money when we are starting out in private practice. I would encourage you to err on the side of being generous with your time and expertise at the outset. Keep in mind that these activities are helping you to become known in your community.

CONTACT PRIVATE PRACTICE PHYSICIANS

This group can be challenging to contact because they are so pressed for time. Taking advantage of a time when they might already be planning to gather to discuss cases will help. So, if you offer to present a case with both medical and neuropsychological features, you increase the likelihood of meeting physicians.

If you really are new in town, you may want to start by contacting the local neuropsychology organization, if there is one. Ask in advance for information about various clinics. You should also find the local neurology organization, to see if their membership is open to other health care providers. Attending their monthly talks, meetings, and dinners is a very good way to begin meeting physicians who are interested in similar clinical issues.

It is also useful to approach individual neurology practitioners, primary care practitioners, mental health departments, or rehabilitation departments of hospitals. Obtain the name of the department chair and send him or her a cover letter with your curriculum vitae and some proposed topics for talks you can present to their staff. Follow up with a phone call. You have nothing to lose. The worst they can say is no.

CONTACT INDEPENDENT NURSE CASE MANAGERS

Independent nurse case managers have often forged strong relationships with case management companies, insurance companies, various medical providers, vocational groups, neuropsychologists, clinical psychologists, everyone on the continuum of care for brain-injured patients. As self-employed people, they are often open to overtures from other private practitioners. Because they manage the many complex cases that come their way, they also benefit from knowing a good source for neuropsychological evaluations, in-service training, and consultation advice in their community.

Call and invite neurology practitioners to lunch. Find out what sorts of cases he or she prefers. Learn if he or she gets neuropsychological evaluations. Find out what psychology or neuropsychology services are needed most and have been the least available. Let him or her know specifically what you are prepared to deliver: For instance, timely evaluation and communication of results via both phone discussion and formal report; cost-effective work; clinically useful reports; and a willingness to testify in court or to be deposed, if necessary. If you have a sample of an evaluation report that offers clear findings and useful treatment recommendations, you may wish to share it (with all identifying information removed, of course, to protect patient confidentiality).

Finally, if you have expertise in working with families who are struggling to cope with changes in their loved one after brain injury, or an interest in providing individual psychotherapy for the patients themselves, let this be known. Psychologists who are trained as both neuropsychologists and psychotherapists are a relatively rare breed–and one in demand.

CONTACT PRIVATE VOCATIONAL FIRMS

Private vocational firms often have many of the same needs and interests as nurse case managers, but with a particular emphasis on return-to-work issues. They want and need neuropsychological reports that help bridge the gap between test performance and predicted real-life potential. These reports should include specific guidelines for how to further assess and manage deficits in a real-life work circumstance, based upon the patient's areas of cognitive or behavioral strength and weakness, as revealed by testing.

Being prepared to advise job coaches or rehabilitation specialists to work most effectively on-site with brain-injured patients is another strong asset. A combination of neuropsychology, clinical psychology, rehabilitation psychology, and practical appreciation for the world of work, supervisors, co-workers, and common adjustment problems will all be selling points with vocational counselors.

ATTEND WEEKLY HOSPITAL TEACHING ROUNDS

If you live or work near a medical school, you might take advantage of the teaching rounds held each week. You can probably find listings on the school's website. You should avail yourself of these opportunities to learn, listen, observe, ask questions, and to become known to your colleagues for your thoughtful inquiries. You will also find this is a good way to get to know who's who within a particular department.

In addition, you will glean helpful information about grants, research projects, or clinical programs that you may later want to pursue with a more formal request for involvement. If you are a good scientist who is willing to assist on a project, to help with database management or other aspects, you may be quite a find. This is a great way to keep yourself active and current in the research domain and to let colleagues get to know you personally.

This kind of involvement can also lead to teaching opportunities. Beginning as a guest lecturer may make it easier later to obtain a clinical or adjunct faculty appointment.

SUPERVISE RESIDENTS, INTERNS, AND POSTDOCTORAL FELLOWS

Although the primary purpose of this supervision is certainly not marketing, it will have indirect marketing effects. You will inevitably have an impact, hopefully positive, upon your trainees. This is one of the ways in which, as you review cases, provide useful feedback and advice, and otherwise support the development of younger peers, your reputation can build and spread.

OBTAIN GRADUATE STUDENT HELP FOR RESEARCH

Publication is an important part of marketing, yet few people in private practice seem to find the time for it. They have good ideas, they are doing direct clinical work, they are making astute observations about various diseases and various kinds of test performance. Yet it is hard to find the time for research when so much is depending upon them financially.

The irony is that private practitioners are usually sitting upon a treasure trove of clinical data. If you recall your graduate school days for just a moment, and the relative scarcity of huge clinical populations to study, you will realize that in your office, a typical four-drawer file cabinet of patient folders may hold enough interesting projects for the next 5 years.

Create a good working relationship with a graduate student who is interested in thesis or dissertation data. In return for helping set up a database, enter data, and run analyses, your student colleague will have access to a clinical population and, therefore, an interesting dissertation. Not only will you have spent time with an enthusiastic and up-to-date junior colleague, you will also have your own database from which to launch a variety of interesting studies. You can continue to write, publish, and do research without taking on the entire burden of data management.

CONFERENCE PARTICIPATION: YOURS AND OTHER RELATED PROFESSIONS

Submitting papers, posters, and other kinds of presentations at your local, regional, and national psychology or neuropsychology association meetings is an other excellent way to market your ideas and services. This is a smaller world than you may realize. People refer from other states. We are all part of a mobile population, and I, for one, am often looking for colleagues in other cities to whom I can refer patients. The national community of neuropsychologists who are organizationally active is a relatively small group of individuals. It is in your best interest on many levels to be a member of the International Neuropsychological Society, of the National Academy of Neuropsychology, and of other professional organizations.

It may be worth your time to agree to lecture at local, national, or international venues, even if there is not substantial remuneration. In addition, be open to accepting speaking invitations from other specialty organizations, such as nursing, speech pathology, occupational therapy, rehabilitation medicine conferences, or neurology meetings.

Not only are these trips worth your time away from your practice, but as a self-employed person it is probably a legitimate tax deduction. Add a little vacation time on to the end of your trip; you may cover your airfare and other legitimate expenses as part of your business travel.

PUBLISH

Journal articles, book chapters, books, manuals, abstracts, and even the popular brain injury press may all be areas where your ideas and writing can find expression. The more workshops and presentations you do, the more likely it is that your work will be known, and people will think of you when they are thinking, for example, of contributors to gather for an edited book.

You don't have to merely wait and hope that someone will like a talk that you give. When you are surveying the literature and see like-minded authors whose data bases or clinical ideas appear to complement your own, contact that author. Learn if he or she might be willing to consider a collaborative project that would, for example, increase the *N* of his or her data; or one that might refine or expand the published findings. This might even launch the two of you into a related area as co-authors.

When in doubt, speak up. The greatest risk of solo practice is isolation. Not only for the vitality of your practice, but also for your mental and intellectual vitality, stay in touch with colleagues, with science and with teaching. It will bring you full circle to doing good work, and you will be building a good reputation.

EXERCISE: MY FIVE PREFERRED MODES OF MARKETING

1. Make a list of the five marketing approaches that are likely to be most effective and most comfortable for you to pursue. For instance, providing in-service training on neuropsychology and rehabilitation topics to nurse case managers at private companies, inviting local physicians or providers to lunch to discuss what you could provide to them, developing and giving a workshop for allied health professionals or attorneys, developing and mailing brochures on your treatment groups or your testing services, contacting providers for whom you have previously worked to offer your services (as long as this is not a conflict of interest with your former employer).

2. Select three items from your list above, and develop a plan for implementation. Schedule a lunch date, an in-service training, and create a brochure for your business. Keep track of the hours your spend within each activity, including all of your preparation time, travel, and in-person contact, and the direct costs associated with each activity (This might include cost of lunch, brochure printing, handouts for inservice).

7

CREATIVE APPROACHES TO FINANCIAL ISSUES

As you establish your practice, you will want to consider creative ways to eliminate, share, or otherwise reduce your operating costs. If you are making the transition from a salaried job, plan in advance for a minimum of one year to make this change. Advance planning will allow you to save money upon which to live for 6 months as well as to begin exploring various practice settings and options.

Having a nest egg is critical. My own plan involved taking three months off prior to resuming work in gradual transition into private practice. At the time I left my institutional job, I didn't know exactly what I would be doing in my private practice or how to craft it. I decided to discover how my interests and opportunities each would evolve when there wasn't so much direct pressure to generate billable hours. I was also willing to do other forms of work if it became necessary to support myself.

During the 3-year period that I had actually been considering a move to self-employment, and while experimenting with an 80% versus 100% time institutional position, I was also able to set the stage for living on less income. I refinanced my house, established a line of credit, and paid my debts. By the time I left my former job, my mortgage was my only debt.

I expected I would be earning at the equivalent of part-time work for some time as my practice grew.

The first cornerstone of my self-employed life was within a nonprofit medical clinic, where I negotiated a .25 appointment as their only neuropsychologist. In return for my 10 hours a week, we agreed that six of those hours would be guaranteed, so that even if patients did not show, I would be paid. The clinic already had a long history of neuropsychological evaluation services. The prior neuropsychologist had taken another job, and they wanted to fill this position. They knew from their own scheduling history that "no shows" were rarely a problem, thanks to good initial screening. The clinic staff did a good job of managing all referrals, scheduling, billing, and collections. The clinic also provided all testing equipment, malpractice insurance, and a dictation service. This work involved no direct overhead expense to me. I averaged 12 hours per week of work. They paid me slightly more than the hourly rate they would have paid a regular salaried employee. I enjoyed seeing elderly patients there that I probably would not have seen in my private practice. Look for a similar mutually beneficial relationship when you explore contractual possibilities.

As I mentioned earlier, I also consulted for a variable number of hours each month as a neuropsychologist with a private rehabilitation company, with an upper limit of 20 hours each month. When those hours were guaranteed, I charged half my usual fee. When the company's fiscal needs changed, the hours were no longer guaranteed, and I charged my usual fee. I then worked an average of 5 hours a month at the higher rate. The company paid promptly when I submitted my monthly bill. We enjoy what has become a long-standing relationship. With periodic review it has changed a number of times, to our continuing mutual satisfaction.

In addition to conducting my private practice, I also wanted to continue to teach and do research. To that end, it became increasingly important to maximize the economic productivity of my clinical time. When you are self-employed, the direct and absolute relationship between how you spend your time and your resulting income becomes very clear.

So, I gradually transitioned from a part-time undergraduate teaching load, which took a tremendous amount of time but paid very little, to conducting more workshops with better reimbursement. I expanded my evaluation practice and satisfied my love of teaching by supervising interns and postdoctoral fellows. I also taught an occasional guest lecture at our medical school, where I had clinical appointments in both psychiatry and in rehabilitation medicine.

I also learned to bill fairly and accurately for the time I actually spent conducting evaluations and preparing the final reports. I initially had a tendency to underestimate my time, in an effort to keep my evaluation prices low. Reviewing records, administering and scoring tests, double-checking details of a Minnesota Multiphasic Personality Inventory, making calls and collateral interviews, and providing feedback to patients and families is a time-consuming process. Make sure you capture those hours in adequate billing.

In an institutional setting, it may be easy to let go of some billing details, as you are protected by the larger, revenue-generating capacities of many departments. I have observed that, in general, practitioners in all settings do not adequately reflect in their billing the actual time they spend on patient care activities. This is worth reviewing from time to time, to see if there are legitimate methods for billing for all your work.

Although some neuropsychologists charge a flat fee for a neuropsychological evaluation, I prefer to set an hourly fee. Some cases are more complex, some are more straightforward, some bring extensive records and prior neuropsychological evaluation reports, some are starting fresh with you. I prefer to bill for my exact time in each circumstance, including for medical-legal evaluation. When you are establishing your practice, I recommend charging an hourly fee, so that, with time, you can develop a sense of what constitutes a full evaluation versus more brief, or more extended, assessments.

TRADING CONSULTATION TIME FOR OFFICE SPACE

When I began to look for office space, I was astonished at how expensive it was and I felt wary about incurring so much overhead before I had any income. Searching for an alternative, I approached a private rehabilitation company, which had a testing space complete with testing equipment. The company was interested in my consulting for their brain injury cases, for staff training, and for the occasional neuropsychological evaluation. We negotiated a day rental rate for the testing room. I only paid for the room if I used it. Since I was also consulting with the company's staff and clients, we kept track of our respective bills, and essentially wound up trading my consultation time for their office space. They had free parking at their building, were in an excellent location, and it was in our both of our best interests to have the testing materials put to good use.

SHARING TESTING MATERIALS

When the Wechsler Adult Intelligence Scale, third edition (WAIS-III) and Wechsler Memory Scale, third edition (WMS-III) became available, I was better established and able to afford their purchase. However, it was not uncommon for my colleagues and me to occasionally lend an instrument to one another. For example, alternate forms of tests, such as, the Fuld Object Memory Test—Form II, an older WMS, the Porteus Mazes, alternate forms of the 12 word Selective Reminding Test with the recognition cards, or other less common tests were only occasionally used by any one examiner. They were ideal for sharing, and allowed us to supplement our respective core batteries without extensive additional expense.

ADVICE ON BILLING AND COLLECTIONS

Certain insurance carriers pay a fair rate for neuropsychological work and others do not. Check with your colleagues in private practice if you do not know how to bill and collect. These conversations can save you endless hours of frustration and lost income.

I had a general understanding of what our state worker compensation carriers covered. I knew a number of self-insured companies, for whom I had done work in my institutional days. I also knew that I did not want to deal with federal government agencies in my private practice. My one experience with a Federal Workers Compensation carrier has done nothing to improve my outlook in this regard.

To avoid confusion regarding bill submission (i.e., does it go to the patient's medical plan or to the mental health plan), I use only medical diagnosis codes in my practice. I use only the following Current Procedural Terminology (CPT) codes in private insurance billing:

- 96115—Neurobehavioral screening evaluation, for brief exams (2–3 hours is typical for me)
- 96117—Neuropsychological evaluation for all time spent in record review, test administration, scoring, interview, and report writing (12 hours is typical)
- 90887—Review of results with patient (typically 1 hour)

For our worker compensation carrier, a somewhat different breakdown is required, and I follow their guidelines:

- 90801—Diagnostic Interview—one unit (1 hour)
- 96117—Neuropsychological Evaluation as above—up to 10 units (10 hours)
- 90887—Review of Results—one unit (1 hour)
- 96100—MMPI administration, scoring and interpretation—one unit (1 hour)

There are additional codes, probably unique to Washington state, for very complex worker compensation cases, where there may be two prior neuropsychological evaluations to review, a very extensive set of medical records, and a tremendous amount of time required to analyze and synthesize the full file. These "M" codes can be used to provide increased and fair reimbursement.

For legal billing, if I know the attorney and know that he or she pays promptly, I will submit a bill after the evaluation has been completed and the report has been filed. Otherwise, I require full payment in advance. A $2,000 retainer is a reasonable fee in my community. Yours may be different. There have been times I did not use the entire amount, and reimbursed the attorney the difference. (See Chapter 8 for more details on medical legal work.)

OBTAINING BASIC DATA FROM YOUR PATIENTS

It is important to have a thorough basic information sheet which lists the patient's name, address, phone numbers, date of birth, Social Security number, driver's license number, name of spouse or significant other, and the name, address, and telephone number of your referral source (see Appendix D for examples of forms). It is also critical to have space for all pertinent insurance information, including the phone number to be called for preauthorization of services.

OBTAINING INSURANCE AUTHORIZATION

Periodically, patients' insurance coverage changes. If this is the result of consolidations or buyouts of their carrier, the patients themselves may not even be aware that their coverage has changed. I always asked my patients' families to check on their policies prior to the appointment, so they would know what was likely to be covered. I always made myself available to speak with insurance companies to clarify a particular point or to provide written documentation of what was planned for the evaluation, but I did not initiate the call.

In part, I wanted the patient and family to understand that they bore the major responsibility in this payment process, and to make them aware of the effort in contacting insurance companies. In some cases, this led patients to change health plans, as they decided to terminate a particular HMO or PPO and to seek out better health plans. In other cases, it led to patients deciding not to spend their resources on a neuropsychological evaluation. I also gave those patients information on institutions that offered evaluations at a slightly lower hourly fee.

CONTRACT AND 50% DOWN FOR PRIVATE NEUROPSYCHOLOGICAL EVALUATION

The insurance companies have no incentive to assist me; they do have some incentive to assist their own paying customers. I learned the hard way over time to collect a sizable copayment in advance from privately insured patients. I do bill their insurance companies but I let the patients or family resolve any differences with their insurance carrier.

I have developed a contract in which patients agree to be responsible for any unpaid balance (see Appendix C). We also agree upon the parameters for this reimbursement ahead of time. Typically they pay a deposit on half of the total estimated cost of the evaluation. I conduct the evaluation, provide a report, and bill their insurance company for the total cost. Once I have received that reimbursement, I will bill the patient for any remaining balance, which is due in 30 days. Or, if the total amount I have been paid exceeds the original bill (e.g., the insurance company paid more than we were expecting, or the total amount of testing was less than anticipated, so the deposit was actually too much), I write the patient a check for the overpayment.

CPT CODES

I always use medical diagnostic codes for my neuropsychological evaluations; I don't take patients for whom there is not a neurologic or medical diagnosis. (See Appendix H for a list of typical International Classification of Diseases, 9th edition [ICD-9] codes.)

I use the 96117 CPT code exclusively to bill the total hours of the neuropsychological evaluation process. Over the years, in discussions with medical or psychology directors for a number of insurance companies, I have learned that many insurance carriers have a "two out of three" rule in place to determine if a bill should be submitted to the patient's mental health or medical plan for reimbursement.

This "two out of three" rule refers to three factors that are considered in determining if the bill should be sent to the medical plan for full reimbursement or to the mental health plan for partial reimbursement. Those three factors are provider's degree (e.g., Ph.D., M.D., ARNP, M.S.W.), ICD-9 diagnostic code, and the CPT code. If two of those three factors are considered mental health variables, the bill will be submitted to the patient's mental health carrier for payment. If two of those three factors are considered medical variables, the bill will be submitted to the patient's medical insurance carrier for payment.

In day-to-day practice I have discovered the following:

1. *The provider variable*: A bill from a psychologist is always categorized as a mental health variable in the "two out of three" decision rule.

2. *The diagnostic code*: If the ICD-9 code listed is a medical code, and if no other nonmedical codes are listed (e.g., depression or adjustment reaction, as secondary diagnoses) the bill is presumed to belong to the medical

insurance plan. If the primary ICD-9 code listed is a mental health code (i.e., Cognitive Disorder NOS is a mental health code), the bill will automatically go to mental health, since a Ph.D. provider plus a mental health ICD-9 code yields two of three factors on the mental health side of reimbursement.

In some cases if you list two diagnostic codes, with the relevant medical code as the primary diagnosis and a psychological code (e.g., reactive depression) as a secondary diagnosis, this latter code and the fact that you are a psychologist may be used to force the entire neuropsychological testing bill, including all of the 96117 hours, over to the mental health plan for 50% reimbursement. This may be true even if the patient is, for example, someone with a brain tumor and no prior mental health history or treatment.

3. *The CPT code*: 96117 is now generally considered a medical plan code for purposes of neuropsychological evaluation. For some insurance companies, if you also include 90801 or 96100 codes as part of your billing (e.g., 90801 for interview, 96117 for neuropsychological testing, 96100 for the MMPI), they will automatically force the entire bill over the to mental health plan for payment.

To reduce confusion and to keep the diagnostic emphasis on the neurologic injury, disease, or problem, I use only 96117 for the CPT code, and only a single, primary medical diagnosis for the ICD-9 coding. The only exceptions to this are the following:

1. Brief neurobehavioral status exams might be given on a screening basis, using 96115 instead of 96117, and saving the 96117 code for a later, full neuropsychological evaluation.

2. Certain insurance companies, for example, Regence, have made it clear they want the 96117 hours submitted to the patient's *medical* insurance plan (reimbursed at 80–90%) and the interview (90801) and MMPI (96100) components billed to the *mental health* plan (reimbursed to the patient at 50% of what is allowed). Preauthorization will need to be obtained from the two separate departments.

3. Washington State Labor and Industries (Washington state's workers' compensation carrier) has a very specific list of codes to be used, where a unit is equivalent to 1 hour. Your state may have different rules. Check with your local colleagues in private practice for this information. In Washington state, one submits billing on a specific government form and separately lists 90801 for 1 unit of interview, 96117 for up to 10 units of neuropsychological testing, a separate code for 1 unit of record review, 96100 for the MMPI (1 unit), another code for review of results or staffing meeting, and some codes unique to this state for complex cases. These "M" codes can provide an additional flat fee reimbursement of about $250 when reviewing extensive records of prior neuropsychological evaluations is part of your own evaluation and consultation in the case.

HOW TO BILL AND COLLECT FOR LEGAL WORK

The best policy is to require prepayment for neuropsychological evaluations conducted as part of a legal case (see Chapter 8 for more on medical legal work). Over time, you may make exceptions to that policy if you know that the attorney will ultimately make the payment, regardless of the outcome of the client's case.

Even attorneys who have every intention of paying what they owe may not mention that they plan to wait until the case settles prior to paying your bill. In many instances, this means that you will wait 1 to 2 years for payment. Some practitioners are willing to take legal work on a lien basis, so that at the time of settlement, they are guaranteed payment. You need to decide how you wish to practice and develop your own payment policy.

It is probably worth noting that in my private practice I have only twice not been paid for neuropsychological evaluations. Once, an attorney did not like my findings, and once a patient discovered belatedly that his insurance carrier would not cover the evaluation.

On another occasion I told an attorney that if I did not receive payment for a delinquent bill I would file a complaint with the state licensing board. I eventually received payment.

These were three highly unpleasant experiences; I learned from them and I hope you can benefit from my experience. In each instance, the attorneys and the patient had been recommended to me by other practitioners. However, it happened that those practitioners had never before reached findings that did not support the attorney's case, and in the latter instance, they had not had any personal dealing with the patient, only contact as rehabilitation colleagues.

Some attorneys will ask you to submit the billing first to the patient's health insurance company, and then send the attorney the unpaid balance. I recommend against this practice. If an evaluation is medically or psychologically necessary for appropriate clinical care of the patient's injury or residual problems, the patient's health providers can initiate the request. If the attorney is initiating the evaluation request, he or she is responsible for the bill.

It is sometimes appropriate to submit the unpaid balance of a clinical neuropsychological evaluation bill to an attorney for payment. For example, when the evaluation is part of the medical expenses deemed to be appropriate for the person's care but is not fully reimbursed by the patient's health insurance or personal injury policy. Attorneys can also cover testing costs if after completion of all clinical treatment the unpaid neuropsychological evaluation is called into testimony and will be used by either the plaintiff or defense to document various issues in the case.

Finally, in all evaluation situations, whether strictly clinical, legal, or a combination of the two, I charge my usual clinical fees ($150 an hour) for record review, interviewing and testing the patient, interviewing family members or other relevant individuals, and preparing and submitting my final report.

I charge $400 an hour for consultations with attorneys (in 15-minute increments) whether by telephone or in person, and $400 an hour for depositions held in my office (with a 2-hour minimum) and for courtroom appearances (with 4-hour minimum). Travel time and expenses are additional. A good rule of thumb for guiding your initial billing framework is to determine how much money you are losing from your practice on that day by being away from the office.

REDUCED COST MALPRACTICE INSURANCE

By arranging a quarter-time contract position as a clinical neuropsychologist at a private clinic, all of my clinical work on their behalf occurs on their premises, with their patients, and is totally covered by their institutional malpractice. As a result, I do not have to carry the cost of full-time malpractice insurance in the number of hours remaining in my private practice. As long as I average less than 15 hours a week with my private patients, I am able to qualify for the reduced rates available to part-time practitioners. The cost difference between full time and part-time malpractice insurance can be substantial.

CONTRACT ASSISTANTS

At various phases of my career, I have either done all of my own testing, a few hours of my own testing with the rest done by two excellent psychometrists, or some combination of these approaches. During the first few years of my solo private practice, I did almost all of my own testing. Later, as my caseload increased, I began to rely more upon the services of a highly experienced psychometrist who was well known to me from prior work in an institutional setting.

In Seattle, psychometrist services can be obtained on a contract basis for $25–$30 an hour. The typical psychometrist time for testing and scoring in my practice is 8 hours, as I do some of the testing and scoring myself. If we have last-minute cancellations, I pay the psychometrist a half-day's salary (4 hours), so her time will not be lost. I also paid an additional $11 per year on my malpractice insurance policy for coverage of her work with me and my patients.

It is also possible to contract with other licensed psychologists to handle overflow business from your practice during particularly busy times or during vacation or professional leave. It is very important to know those psychologists well, and for everyone to be very clear on the extent, limits, and requirements of the business agreement. This arrangement does not work for everyone, of course. I met with an attorney to review the legal issues involved in such an arrangement, and then I created an agreement with two other self-employed neuropsychologists whose work and clinical skills I like and respect, and whose integrity is peerless. They were also solo practitioners and wanted to gradually develop a combination of activities, including increased evaluation work.

The basic agreement we developed included the following points. Please note that these items do not constitute legal advice. You should always check carefully with your own attorney and with payors and referring providers, to ensure the legality of contracted employees.

1. We each maintain our own separate businesses and our own separate referral sources, and each carry our own malpractice insurance for these separate, individual practices.
2. I also added each of them to my malpractice insurance as part-time or occasional contract employees for my private practice. This cost me an additional $11 per year per person.
3. I handled all of the office work—incoming referrals, all calls, scheduling, billing, collections, correspondence, and payment of any and all overhead associated with these patients. This included paying the psychometrist, the transcriptionist, the courier, and paying for office supplies, as well as paying the psychologists an established hourly fee.
4. They agreed to accept payment from me for their time when the bill was paid by the insurance company. I agreed to submit those bills in a timely manner, to pay the psychologists our agreed-upon hourly rate within 5 working days of receiving payment, and to insure the evaluation services were preauthorized before scheduling the patients with these practitioners.
5. Both practitioners also agreed not to solicit referrals from my referral sources and if subsequently contacted directly by a referral source for whom they had done work via my company, to see the patient under the auspices of my private practice.
6. Each of us had the right to terminate the contract with 30 days written notice.
7. None of us had the right to solicit referrals from anyone else's referral sources.

Since we all work in the same city, at times we had had prior independent referrals from, for example, the same group of vocational counselors. We agreed to remain with the referring individuals we knew prior to the agreement. If new referrals were made from someone in the referral group other than our ordinary contact, we would try to ascertain if it was intended for us personally, or if it more properly belonged to one of the other two neuropsychologists. This plan has worked well for us. It would probably not work well for everyone. As a result of our arrangement, my colleagues have seen some interesting additional cases that they might not otherwise have seen. I was able to maintain a continuous flow of referrals to my practice without an undue waiting list or without extended downtime or absences because of travel. And we have enjoyed discussing cases with one another. That is an opportunity is not otherwise easily built into daily business.

One final insurance note on using contract neuropsychologists. If you would like to keep this as option open for you in your own practice, it will be important to be clear with insurance companies that although you are an individual practitioner, your business also has contract employees. Therefore, similar to local hospitals, clinics, and medical centers, you will be billing under one name (your company name) and one tax identification number (the company's Federal Tax ID number) but conceivably for a number of different providers, each of whom will need their own provider number with that insurance company.

It is very important that the insurance company has the proper database linkage between each of the providers and their various business or billing addresses. For example, I was a specific provider for neuropsychological evaluations done at a private medical center in my quarter time job. Work done there was billed by that clinic, and reimbursement was sent to them at their business address. The clinic then paid me an hourly fee for my time.

When I billed some of those same companies directly from my private practice, they were confused, since the clerk processing the bill had not noticed that the bill was on my private practice letterhead, with a different tax ID number, and a different address for service. You need to be explicit with insurance companies, both at the time of preauthorization, as well as during billing and collection phases, especially if you are expanding into private practice after being institution based.

Also, recognize these companies need to have both—or all—of your addresses listed in their database, with notations that there is more than one billing address for you as a provider. Simply noting this on your letterhead or bill will not solve the problem. You must contact them directly, preferably in writing and with a follow-up phone call or email, to confirm.

In similar fashion, your contract neuropsychologists need to alert all companies for whom they are reimbursed that these psychologists are now employed by two separate companies who may bill for their work: their own private practice and, now, your practice.

Payment for services should always be made to your company, under your federal tax ID number, since it is your business that is generating the referrals, having the patients seen, paying salaries and expenses. To establish a fair hourly rate of pay for the contract neuropsychologists, I calculated my average collection rate then calculated the average time and overhead involved in my setting up these particular referrals, and I paid the contract neuropsychologists the difference.

If these neuropsychologists wished to use a psychometrist, I made those arrangements as well. I paid the psychometrist immediately for his or her time, and later I deducted an agreed-upon proportion of that amount from the neuropsychologist's paycheck.

TAX DEDUCTIONS, A GOOD ACCOUNTANT AND TYPE OF BUSINESS

Perhaps for the first time in your life, you will be filing a heavily itemized tax return, and it is absolutely worth your time and the added expense of an accountant to do so (see Appendix K for a listing of possible deductions). With any luck, you will become meticulous and thoughtful as you plan your travel time, conference time, expenses, purchases for the business, and, if appropriate, the expenses of a home office.

You should speak to an accountant, and if needed, an attorney, about the advantages, requirements and limitations of a sole proprietorship, a partnership, or of incorporation. You may decide to start out as a sole proprietor, and later decide to form a corporation. Sound legal and fiscal advice is important in this process, and later, for appropriate preparation of tax returns.

EXERCISE: PRACTICAL PLANNING

1. *What do you plan to charge for your services?*
2. *What monthly net income do you need?*
3. *What are your direct expenses each month?*
4. *How much gross income do you therefore need?*
5. *How many hours will you need to bill and collect?*
6. *What teaching, contract, or other supplemental sources of income do you have, in addition to revenue generated each month from your private practice?*
7. *Run the numbers, in each area, and see if there are ways to further reduce your fixed expenses, at least for the first year. If you can, you'll also reduce your stress.*

8

MEDICAL–LEGAL WORK

THE PROBLEMS WITH LEGAL WORK

In the typical medical–legal referral circumstance, you are asked to evaluate and sometimes to testify about the presence, absence, and degree of brain impairment present in an individual, following injury or illness. Although one hopes that the judge will be fair, keep in mind that the attorneys involved are not expected to be neutral or fair. Their job is not to seek justice; they represent the interests of their clients. They have been hired as advocates for their clients, and not as advocates of what we may consider an objectively reasonable neuropsychological truth.

The plaintiff's attorney seeks to secure as much reimbursement as possible for his or her client, justified by the injury or loss they may have suffered. The defendant's attorney seeks to protect the financial and legal interests of the person or company being sued. These attorneys' livelihoods depend upon winning cases, or upon negotiating settlements that deliver optimal outcomes to their clients, and therefore, to themselves. Attorneys are typically paid a substantial percentage of a settlement they collect, or they are paid salaries or hourly fees from the companies who employ them.

Whether or not it is explicit, attorneys are looking to you for scientific and clinical support of their positions. They are not interested in data that do not support their position.

Nonetheless, your job is to present the most accurate review of the neuropsychological data that you can determine. Yet unlike the typical clinical circumstance, your conclusions regarding possible deficits and their implications for function in day-to-day life are likely to have a direct bearing on large amounts of money being lost by one side or gained by another.

As a result, the patient and his representatives or defendants and their representatives may bring significant pressure to bear upon you to view your data with a particular emphasis. This pressure and the accompanying adversarial process can be unpleasant. I encourage you to charge fees that compensate you for both the level of stress you may feel, as well as for the value of your work.

TRUE BELIEVER POLEMICS IN THE ABSENCE OF STRONG SCIENTIFIC DATA

In response to these pressures, you may have observed, either in yourself or others, that legal work can promote the development of entrenched opinions on the part of expert witnesses. When anyone's opinions are scrutinized in an adversarial and potentially hostile atmosphere, it is not easy to maintain equanimity about the facts.

Further, when one's opinions are challenged, it is natural to maintain even more rigorously a particular point of view. Yet your honestly derived perspectives may reflect a clinical reality that has substantial room for doubt. But in the harsh light of the courtroom, you will be asked to speak in terms of probabilities, not possibilities. In doing so, you may not feel able to adequately qualify your opinions.

The pressure to render possibilities into probabilities can sometimes be very subtle. It may even become an alluring consideration in the hands of a charming, articulate, and passionate attorney. Haven't we all wanted someone to advocate for us so well and so effectively? Ministers, attorneys, and some psychologists share a certain set of personality tendencies—to rely heavily on verbal and emotional powers of persuasion, to delight in the well-turned phrase, and to dazzle with a brilliance that can be hammered into clarity and then press the point home. Sound like fun? If it does, you may be particularly vulnerable to getting swept up in the drama of it all. You may need to be careful to not resort to the kind of advocacy that sometimes masquerades as professionally appropriate testimony.

INTEGRITY AND REPUTATION—ARE YOU A PLAINTIFF OR A DEFENSE EXPERT?

If a significant portion of your salary depends upon courtroom testimony, which does ultimately translate into helping attorneys win cases, I believe that over time, you will find it increasingly difficult to be open-minded and objective. It is not that money itself can make you testify to opinions you don't actually believe. The problem is you are repeatedly rewarded for expressing an opinion that you already hold. With repeated testimony, that opinion becomes more strongly embedded, even if developing research evidence or courtroom discoveries suggest a modification of your opinion. If that modified opinion renders your testimony more neutral, if your opinions become less absolute, you will likely be in less demand as a witness. Consider how this will affect the integrity of your work if your income will be significantly threatened or reduced.

POTENTIAL WAR OF THE CLINICAL AND LEGAL WORLDS

Clinical realities and legal requirements often serve different masters. When those worlds truly intersect, something useful may occur that is also reflective of scientific facts as we know them. However, if there is much room for disagreement about the facts, or interpretation of the facts, their current impact or long-term implications for the patient and the costs of treatment, one's conclusions may be called into question. In those circumstances, it is difficult to avoid some small particle of defensiveness about your opinions.

Legal work is risky on several levels. It may damage your reputation. It may make you cynical about the judicial process. But probably most dangerous for the scientist-practitioner, legal work as an expert witness can begin to limit your ability to form objective opinions.

This vulnerability is not likely to result from a conscious decision on your part to take a particular position, "independent of the facts." Instead, this bias is more likely to occur over time as part of a subtle alteration in your attitude toward a particular group of patients or clinical problems. Hence, you begin to develop a preliminary bias. You tend either to believe or to doubt the clinical presentation consistent with your bias. This may affect your appreciation of the patient's actual strengths or true deficits; this can also result in an overly restricted or exaggerated view of various possible modifying factors.

Repeated exposure to unsympathetic patients whose injuries do not limit their ability to return to work, but who prefer not to work ever again, or contact with attorneys with questionable ethics, or confronted with insurance companies whose intent is to completely minimize rather than acknowledge the actual extent of an injury can all lead you to develop a jaded outlook, when the spirit of scientific inquiry and steadiness is needed instead. Entering into the forensic world of smoke and mirrors inevitably alters your view of the proceedings and your role in them. Nonscientific or nonclinical influences that are part of colorful courtroom theatre may begin to exert greater distortion on your opinions than the quiet and less colorful observations that result from scientific research and clinical observation.

Acknowledging these problems doesn't mean that you should never do forensic work; it does mean that you must develop increased vigilance to limit the effects of these problems upon your professional judgments. There are also other factors to keep in mind.

SUBTLE INFLUENCE AND EXAMINER DRIFT

We all know individuals whose expertise or testimony has led them to become professional witnesses. This phenomenon is not a healthy development for neuropsychology nor for any scientifically based field. In all fairness to people who usually find themselves as plaintiff experts, or usually as defense experts, their institutional context must be taken into account. For example, if you are a neuropsychologist in an outpatient brain injury rehabilitation program, you will likely evaluate many patients with severe traumatic brain injury. Many of these cases may eventually go to trial as a result of the accident that caused the injuries. If you have evaluated the patient as part of your program work, you will likely be called to testify about the patient's deficits and recommended treatments. Hence you are likely to be called by the patient's attorney and you will be a plaintiff's expert.

If you are a neuropsychologist in a tertiary care setting, where patients are routinely sent for second or third opinions, you are likely to find yourself doing a preponderance of defense work. The reason the patient was referred to your clinic is usually because someone isn't satisfied with the first opinion. Often the person requesting a second opinion may feel the problems or their long term implications were over-stated in the initial report. Or, they simply want to insure that two reasonable providers agree on the major issues.

Those situations can be tough enough for the practitioners involved, with lots of records and with differing opinions to review. Nonetheless, you will be required to form your conclusions to the best of your ability. In the end, however, one side—the plaintiff or the defense—will lose. Someone will be unhappy with your conclusions.

INADVERTENT PROMOTION OF A LITIGIOUS ZEITGEIST

Over the last 10 to 15 years, I have observed a significant increase in the number of patients with mild or questionable traumatic brain injuries who are referred for evaluation. Frequently, these patients are involved in a lawsuit seeking money for damages sustained from their accidents.

This may be because, in part, increased clinical and scientific appreciation has developed for the types of actual mild residual neuropsychological effects that a small percentage of at-risk concussion patients may suffer. Some of these patients have actually sustained a more serious mild injury (that is, 20 minutes of frank loss of consciousness versus a brief alteration in mental state that did not involve loss of consciousness, or signs of clear brain damage on subsequent MRI). Some patients may also be at increased risk for acquired deficits secondary to age or prior injury or illness.

In neither case, however—the mild injury vs. the complicated mild injury—is the person rendered permanently incapable of full-time employment. However, the willingness of some psychologists to testify about the presence of serious brain damage and inability to work in patients for whom nonneurologic factors play a primary role may have added to the increased frequency of litigation for mild postconcussive injuries.

The literature on the role of litigation in recovery and return to work after possible or actual concussive injuries is somewhat mixed. In the individual clinical case, when patients appear to be functioning far worse than one would predict on the basis of their injuries, it seems that application of W.J. Fordyce's "green poultice"—monetary compensation—may be required before improvement on test scores or in life's activities will be seen.

THE BENEFITS OF FORENSIC WORK

You probably didn't expect to see a subheading on the benefits of forensic work after the preceding cautionary notes, but there are some. They include the following:

1. *Opportunity for ongoing education and mutual peer review.* Doing forensic work provides an interesting opportunity to learn more about how other professionals conduct their evaluations and present their findings. This is true not only for other neuropsychologists, but also seeing how other professionals conduct their workups, including emergency room physicians and staff, neurosurgeons and neurologists, psychiatrists, vocational rehabilitation counselors, life care planners, and speech pathologists. You will have the opportunity to learn the details of a thorough exam, as well as to

appreciate how subtle errors or omissions may occur. You will learn from other clinicians' mistakes.

It is always instructive to discover how other neuropsychologists conduct their evaluations and present their findings. For example, you may learn more about certain tests that you don't typically use. You may be inspired to explore them further. You may discover aspects of report formats that you decide to include in your own reports.

You may also observe stylistic approaches or responses that you don't want to emulate. You will then be better prepared to guard against these problems in your own evaluations, analyses, reports, and testimony.

When another neuropsychologist's review of your work has raised questions or concerns, you have an opportunity to think critically about your own work. You may or may not agree after you have considered the critique, but you will have learned by your openness to it. It is valuable to have periodic review in this fashion. In most clinical situations, there is little time or opportunity for feedback from our peers. However, in a forensic case, experts on the other side are looking for deficits in your neuropsychological argument. Often, they are not nice about how they express this, but their enthusiastic approach has the potential to lead to refinements in your future work if you accept the opportunity. Or, the review may confirm that your approach is the best approach.

One minor cautionary note: It doesn't benefit our profession to make disparaging remarks about opposing experts. One can strongly disagree with someone's conclusions without treating them disrespectfully. Participating wholeheartedly in an adversarial atmosphere may be entertaining or even briefly satisfying at the time, but it is ultimately demeaning to the profession of neuropsychology, and to its representatives—us.

2. *Luxury of testing time and thoroughness*. In a forensic circumstance, you have the luxury to fully explore the range of the patient's talents and difficulties and to refine questions about cognitive and personality function. Your responsibility is to be thorough and to address all the pertinent issues. You are not limited to a brief or modified battery as you might otherwise be in a clinical circumstance of limited time or funding. Instead, you may enjoy this opportunity, for example, to compare a range of appropriate memory tests, while also directly serving the intent of the evaluation.

In the process of forensic work, and the subsequent research on test statistics, we also have the opportunity to learn more about a range of patients and the meaningfulness of particular test scores and parameters. For example, Amin and Prigatano (1993) in their paper on the Hiscock Digit Memory Test, challenged the assumption that chance levels of responding were required to conclude that nonneurologic factors were operating in test performance. Instead, they discovered a very subtle but statistically significant difference in test performance between nonlitigating patients, whether with dementia or severe traumatic brain injury (TBI), versus litigating patients with reported mild TBI. The patients with documented severe brain injury or disease achieved close to 100% correct on this exam. The mildly injured litigating patients were more likely to achieve percentiles in the low to mid 90s. Without a comparison group of neuropsychological test scores from both mildly injured patients in litigation and more severel brain damaged patient, an extremely useful shift in our understanding of chance levels of responding may not have been so clearly seen.

3. *No wrangling with managed care.* In addition to fair reimbursement for your forensic services, you don't have to spend time dealing with insurance companies about preauthorization and payment of your services. You also don't have to accept a reduced payment. If you have handled yourself properly with the law firm for whom you are providing expert testimony, you don't have to chase the company for your money. You also don't get caught in the intracompany battles about where a neuropsychology bill belongs (i.e., in the medical or the mental health benefits). The sheer amount of time spent by you or your staff on the phone, submitting documents to justify testing, asking the primary care provider to send in a letter of support, and so on, is mercifully avoided. This benefit alone may make you consider becoming a forensic expert.

4. *Acknowledgement of your expertise.* You have worked long and hard to achieve your level of knowledge and experience. College, graduate school, practicum experiences, a year long internship, and a year or two of postdoctoral study constitutes a significant amount of time, energy, effort, dedication, and sacrifice. It is satisfying to know a lot about something as vital as the human brain and mind and to be in demand for your skills.

Often, when one is laboring away in one's daily practice, regardless of setting, you may not receive much acknowledgement or appreciation that would be commensurate with your ongoing contributions. Usually, your peers are working as relentlessly as you are, and while focused on patient care or paying the office rent no one has time to think about each other. Forensic work can provide a more public forum for you to demonstrate your talents and to achieve recognition.

5. *Learning something about our judicial system.* Hopefully, you haven't spent a lot of time in court on the wrong side of the witness stand. For most of us, unless we have been arrested or sued, we are not going to get much exposure to judicial proceedings. Perhaps I am mistaken, but it is my impression that psychologists are rarely selected for jury duty. We may be called, but we are quickly culled.

6. *Doing forensic work provides additional educational opportunity.* This can include knowing when *not* to offer additional information if it isn't requested. Forensic work will surely help you learn to keep your temper. You may even learn to develop a greater sense of perspective and increased maturity in the process.

SPINE-FIRMING EXERCISES

Repeat the following words of wisdom prior to testifying:

1. *"I don't know," or "It is not possible to determine that from this information." (Being an expert doesn't imply the need to know answers to unanswerable questions... Or to questions you don't know the answer to.)*
2. *I will not lose my temper.*
3. *I will maintain an even tone of voice.*
4. *I will take my time to think and respond.*
5. *I will ask for questions to be clarified if I don't understand them.*
6. *I will not volunteer information unless it is critical to understanding my point.*
7. *I will be thoroughly prepared.*
8. *I will remain focused on the primary issues and not be distracted by obfuscating and unrelated discussions with the attorney.*
9. *I will not take provocative remarks personally.*
10. *I will not be upset by the lousy way attorneys may treat one another, or witnesses, in any proceeding. The attorneys will probably be dining together when the lunch recess comes, or playing golf on the weekends, while you are still troubled by courtroom histrionics (hopefully, not your own). It is up to the judge to curtail bad behavior if you are in court. It is probably best for you to ignore it and remain above the dramatic fray. Hang tough.*

9

CONSULTATION AND SUPERVISION PRACTICE

An important component of your private practice in neuropsychology may include consultation and supervision services. These are advisory services that can be provided to psychologists or health care providers.

These services can vary from the sporadic or occasional consultation to an ongoing supervisory or consulting relationship. In addition to working with individual clinicians, you may also wish to develop consultation groups with a specific clinical focus.

In some instances, consultation is arranged for a fee. At other times, it may be in your best interest to establish a less formal but long term mutually beneficial relationship with other psychologists, physicians, and health care providers. They will naturally turn to you for free discussion of neuropsychology questions, but will also send their patients to you. Hence you will be building your evaluation practice by being available to educate and assist colleagues in managing their patients with neurologic injury or illness.

There are several practitioner groups with whom you may wish establish contact in this regard, providing both education and marketing that leads to a consulting relationship.

CLINICAL PSYCHOLOGISTS, PRIMARY CARE PHYSICIANS, NURSE PRACTITIONERS, PHYSICIAN ASSISTANTS, AND NEUROLOGY OR REHABILITATION NURSES

These groups of clinicians have typically had either training in psychometric techniques or exposure to basic neurologic principles, respectively, in their professional development. As a result of this training, psychologists, physicians, nurse practitioners, physician assistants, and some registered nurses are likely familiar with cognitive and neurobehavioral changes that are associated with brain dysfunction.

For example, they may recognize the constellation of symptoms associated with the residual effects of traumatic brain injury (TBI) or with dementing conditions, even if neuropsychology or neurology is not an area of specialty. These clinicians are often faced with managing neuropsychological problems in one of several clinical circumstances.

In one circumstance, a patient with a known neurologic disorder is referred for psychotherapy to assist in managing a emotional or behavioral problem, such as depression or anxiety. The behavioral symptoms may or may not be directly related to the underlying medical problem. However, in order to fully maximize the effectiveness of treatment, the clinical psychologist needs to know as much as possible about the patient's cognitive abilities and difficulties.

The clinician might also need guidance and practical suggestions about how best to present therapy information to the patient who has cognitive problems. In this way, the clinical psychologist increases the likelihood that his or her therapeutic interventions will be understood, recalled, and integrated into real behavioral change. This is likely to have a positive long-term effect upon the success of his or her practice because of improved patient function and the appreciation of referring clinicians. This outcome can also extend to maintenance of managed care contracts for the clinician who demonstrates good outcomes.

Further, this clinical psychologist may want to learn more about the signs and symptoms of neuropsychological deficit associated with other neurologic disorders. In this way, he or she can learn to screen more effectively and refer more appropriately in the future.

These clinical psychologists may do basic diagnostic screening on their own, as part of their initial work-up. They don't typically perform full batteries of intellectual and personality assessment, but are often familiar with core instruments, such as the Wechsler Scales, Trail Making A and B, and the MMPI.

Teaching psychologists about the clinical implications of patterns of neurologic impairment seen on testing, and teaching them which particular tests have been found to reveal useful information, will help those clinicians make better referrals for neuropsychological services. This discussion can include a summary review of the literature and the psychometric, neuroanatomic, neuropathologic, and neuroradiologic issues for diagnostic groups that may be of particular interest to the psychologist.

When providing consultation to physicians the situation often includes discussing patients with known neurologic problems who receive their general medical care from an internist or family medicine doctor. It is to this physician that the patient or patient's family are likely to mention cognitive or behavioral problems.

Initially, to establish contact with such practitioners, you may offer a brief in-service training at one of their departmental meetings on a particular diagnostic group with a particular focus on the typical cognitive and neurobehavioral symptoms.

Describing the role of neuropsychological assessment in the long-term management of such patients fits well within this training format. For example, through case example, you can illustrate the value of knowing the patient's level of overall intellectual ability, areas of impairment, and the role of personality and emotional factors in managing the impairment.

Finally, although neuropsychologists do not provide medical advice, our clinical experience and knowledge of the literature may teach us which particular medications are beneficial for cognitive, emotional, and neurobehavioral management of brain injured patients. When you are discussing neuropsychological problems with physicians you may help them refine the range of medications they may be considering for their patients.

NEUROPSYCHOLOGISTS WHO WISH TO AUGMENT THEIR TRAINING

Another practitioner group within your community likely to benefit from consultation is neuropsychologists with strong neuroanatomy, neuropathology, and psychometric backgrounds, but whose therapy skills need development. If you have good psychotherapy skills, you might want to develop this market. With your knowledge of neurologic populations and their impairments, as well as your knowledge of psychotherapeutic principles and techniques, you are in a good position to provide consultation to colleagues who would benefit from both didactic presentations and case supervision.

The didactic format can often be offered most efficiently in a small group seminar. This is also a good way for colleagues to get to know you and perhaps to interest them in pursuing individual consultation. Preparing handouts, references, and teaching cases is also an efficient and productive use of your time. Finally, when several interested professionals are meeting together, it can raise the quality and energy of the discussion.

Depending upon the needs of the practitioner who has requested it your consultation may include a detailed review of specific patients and their neuropsychological problems, but with a particular emphasis upon those patients' emotional and characterologic strengths and vulnerabilities. Consultation may also include continuing discussions of psychotherapeutic interventions that you recommend as well as periodic monitoring of patients progress.

A consultation practice may also entail a broader discussion of clinical and psychotherapy issues. This might include readings in the psychotherapy literature that are relevant to the colleagues' patients. You might also invite guest speakers to attend the occasional group meeting to lead the discussion of particular areas such as object relation or boundary problems of personality disorders.

Perhaps psychotherapy is not one of your primary areas of expertise. There are still likely to be plenty of opportunities for your neuropsychological consultation in the professional community.

For example, if your training was strongly focused upon the science of neuropsychology, you may wish to develop a neuropsychology seminar for neuropsychologists in your community. Neuropsychologists are often looking for convenient opportunities to maintain and develop their skills. State and local psychology organizations do not always fulfill this particular need, but you might.

Your weekly consultation or seminar offerings might include review of a different disease topic and its attendant neuroanotomical, neurofunctional, cellular, and neuropsychological changes. In addition, you could also review particular neuropsychological testing instruments and their psychometric properties such as the standardization of the Wechsler Adult Intelligence Scale III and The Wechsler Memory Scale III, and how they compare to the WAIS-Revised (WAIS-R) and WMS-Revised (WMS-R). You might discuss new instruments and the emerging literature regarding their use.

Topics might range widely to include the latest use of functional magnetic resonance imaging (fMRI), the state of the art in surgical techniques for treating Parkinson's disease, or genetic discoveries related to Alzheimer's disease. Members of the group can also be assigned topics, much as they might in a graduate school seminar. It is your responsibility to then act as a discussant of that topic and to be well informed, with further recommendations for readings, courses, or other training opportunities.

In this fashion, you are being paid directly for your own needed expenditure of time and effort in reading, continuing education, and accumulated experience. You also contribute to the profession as a whole by raising the level of training and expertise.

THERAPISTS IN SOCIAL WORK, COUNSELING, OR PASTORAL COUNSELORS

Although this group of practitioners has not typically had much if any exposure to psychometric and testing principles, they are often in a unique position to observe behavioral and cognitive problems in their patients or clients. They will benefit from a review of common acquired neurologic problems, especially if you include concrete examples of changes they might notice in a patient with a particular injury or illness. Guidelines for referral for neuropsychological testing or neurology consultation can be a valuable tool in the clinical armamentarium of these therapists.

Depending on the setting in which they work, specific consultation or training about various diagnostic subgroups can be useful. For example, counselors who treat alcohol abuse may not be familiar with nonalcohol-related dementia problems. Yet they may work in a setting where older adults are referred for alcohol abuse treatment. It would be important for the therapist to be alert to signs of cognitive or behavioral change that may signal a more global change in function, one which might not be explained solely on the basis of an alcohol history. And of course, alcohol-related cognitive and behavioral problems are important for such counselors to understand.

It is also useful for these practitioners to understand cognitive rehabilitation strategies, especially if you can teach them practical tips for helping their patients cope with memory problems, which will maximize counseling effectiveness.

Organizations, whether a department in a clinic or a freestanding professional group, often have funds available for speakers, and it is appropriate to inquire if they do. Even if it is only a small honorarium, which may not even cover your preparation or copying costs, remember that you are essentially being paid to market your knowledge and expertise to this group of potential referrals. If you are generous with your time, with your handouts, and with your availability by phone to answer questions, you may receive referrals. If only one referral a year comes from this particular effort, income from your work will amply reimburse the time and expense of your talk.

Social workers: Hospital-based social workers may be assisting with the discharge plans of many patients with neurologic problems. These patients may be returning home to their local communities and may need testing or follow-up. However, many patients want to access services that don't involve a long trip back to the hospital. If the social workers know that you are a good resource in a particular part of the county or community, they can include your name in the list of resources provided to the patient, whether for evaluation or treatment or family education services.

REHABILITATION THERAPISTS—OCCUPATIONAL THERAPISTS, PHYSICAL THERAPISTS, SPEECH PATHOLOGISTS, VOCATIONAL COUNSELORS, REHABILITATION SPECIALISTS, RECREATIONAL THERAPISTS, AND CASE MANAGERS

Almost all of these therapists or managers have direct involvement with brain dysfunctional patients and their families. Most of them also need to fulfill continuing education requirements or have a periodic need for individual consultation on difficult or complex cases.

To make yourself known to these practitioners, you might contact their professional organizations to see how their particular speakers' bureau or local in-services may be organized. I may negotiate with people for a small honorarium, just to cover copying and travel costs. You need to use your own judgment about this. Ask whether everyone in the community does this for free, or is an honorarium reasonable?

Agreeing to speak for little or no fee allows you the chance to meet many people at once in a particular professional group. It also allows you to determine if these are people with whom you would welcome future contact. It may also be a good time to see if there are particular individuals with whom you would like to establish a closer working relationship, so you know where to send your patients when they need those services.

Have handouts available on the topic you present as well as a printed list of topics that you would be willing to discuss at future in-services, conferences, or workshops. If you have a website or email address, list those, too. Bring a folder of handouts that includes your business card.

Also, including an evaluation form that needs to be completed to earn continuing education credits is a good way to get feedback about your teaching strengths and weaknesses. You can invite suggestions for future lecture topics as well.

CONSULTATION WITH PSYCHOLOGISTS PREPARING FOR LICENSURE

Consultation groups for licensing candidates can be cost effective for them, and a satisfying opportunity for professional interaction, teaching, and reimbursement for you. However, consider carefully before you take on the professional liability that a *primary* supervisory relationship of the candidates' clinical cases can involve, unless your liability is covered by an institution, or unless the trainee is actually your employee, and therefore covered by your malpractice insurance.

It is stimulating and refreshing to be around people who are fresh from their academic and clinical training, and who are eager to develop their skills. In addition, the time you spend with them doesn't involve adding more patients or more reports to your workload.

Charging reduced fees to such trainees when they are seen as part of a small supervision group yields a modest income each time you meet, with no managed care to negotiate and it provides a valuable service to them.

In addition, it can sometimes be helpful for trainees to have an "off-campus" supervisor or consultant who is not going to sit in judgment of their performance, but who can discuss and advise in a more relaxed atmosphere.

Finally, case discussions that your supervisees bring for review can also add to your own knowledge base. As is so often the case when one is teaching, questions arise that merit further checking. You can assign this follow-up task to the supervisee, also do your own checking, and compare notes at the next meeting. This adds to everyone's growth and updated knowledge.

EXERCISES

List the kind of consultation activities that are most appealing to you and for which you feel well qualified.

List possible local opportunities and contacts for these venues.

Send letters offering services to schools, clinics, and professional organizations.

Advertise via print ads in your state psychological association newsletter the types of services that you offer.

10

PSYCHOMETRIC CONCERNS

A number of practical concerns and issues should be foremost in your mind to help you perform the optimal neuropsychological evaluation. If neuropsychology is your specialty, whether in private practice or other settings, you should be thinking about the issues discussed in this chapter.

THE INTERVIEW: WHO SHOULD BE PRESENT AND WHY?

In general, for a number of reasons, I prefer to initially meet and interview patients in the company of their spouses or other key family members. I think it is best for patients and families to simultaneously hear as I describe the nature, limits, and options of the neuropsychological evaluation process. I hope to demystify the process. Because we are all together, I am assured that everyone has heard the same explanation. In this way, I also communicate that I expect the patient and the family to be open with me and to be mutually involved in resolving problems. I always offer the patient the opportunity to subsequently speak with me alone.

Because of brain damage, patients may not recall what I have said or they may have misperceived or misunderstood what I said. I hope this will be brought to my attention sooner rather than later. Misunderstanding will be clarified or resolved more easily if family members are present. They can reinforce the patient's understanding by reviewing basic facts at home at the end of the day.

The initial interview also provides a valuable opportunity to learn more about the patient's current relationship with his or her family and to observe interpersonal behaviors. Family members' verbal and nonverbal reactions may provide salient information about the impact the patient has had on the family, such engendering fear or an end to patience.

Professionals don't always hear the family's perspective about the patient, yet family members typically have the most accurate, long-term perspective on the patient's premorbid function. In addition, the family is living day-to-day with the patient's alterations in function, some of which are neurologically based and some of which are psychological reactions to deficits. Close family members are likely to have noticed and can often report more accurately than can the patient if changes have occurred in the patient's demeanor, interests, activities, awareness, and behavior.

At the interview, with everyone in the room, I ask the patient's permission to speak independently to family members, and I inform everyone about the nature and limits of confidentiality. I certainly view the patient as my primary focus and commitment, and extend them every right of privacy, as long as it does not countermand their safety, or my ability to practice appropriately on the patient's behalf. This frees me to comment upon areas of concern without being bound by family secrets. I try to be tactful; for example, if there have been changes in sexual function, my report doesn't describe it in excruciating detail. But I need to know about those changes in function (for example whether there is a decrease in desire, difficulty maintaining erections, or hypersexuality). In this way, I can better understand the patient's experience and the implications, both neuroanatomically and interpersonally.

At the interview, I also obtain permission from the patient or family to order additional records that may be helpful to the patient's care. In this way, they are alerted to the release of information requests she or he will be asked to sign, as well as the purpose of the request.

Finally, while the family is present, I schedule a follow-up appointment for review of test results. This facilitates the coordination of everyone's schedules, and ensures that we have an opportunity to discuss findings and a treatment plan as soon as possible after testing.

THE COLLATERAL INTERVIEWS: WHEN, WHY, AND WITH WHOM?

Although interviewing the patient and a key family member is usually sufficient for most clinical situations, in forensic cases or when there are job-related problems of immediate concern, I also request permission to speak with the patient's work supervisor or other relevant individuals. This allows me to obtain information about the patient's strengths and weaknesses in work, or at other settings.

I also request permission to contact previous or current physicians or therapists—or any other relevant individuals. In addition, there are times when patients arrive alone, unaccompanied by their spouse. If so, I arrange for telephone interview with the spouse to collect their comments and observations. If adult children of older patients are available, I also obtain permission to speak with them.

All of these strategies serve the purpose of better understanding the patient and his or her premorbid as well current problems, and it allows for a range of perspectives that can deepen my appreciation for the clinical problems.

There are times when an employer or a co-worker is not at liberty to speak with me or it may not be in the patient's best interest for the employer to be contacted. If so, I try to obtain as much information as I can from the patient and family or perhaps from a friend with whom the patient has previously worked.

PREPARING THE PATIENT TO BE TESTED

The natural anxiety patients bring to the testing situation can often be ameliorated if patients understand the context in which their test performances will be evaluated. For example, I explain that performance on these tests is not like performance on tests in school, where they might expect to obtain 90–100% correct if they have been good students. They may make quite a few errors on a neuropsychological test and still be performing extremely well since making errors may be an expected part of that particular test.

I also explain that IQ scores they received as children in school may be very different from the scores they obtain now, even if their skills have not changed. Differences in IQ scores or other percentile ranks should not automatically be interpreted as a sign of decline or impairment; differences in the tests themselves, in scoring and in comparison groups, as well as in the purposes for which the tests were developed can all contribute to very different results.

I explain that neuropsychological tests measure a range of skills, and that everyone has naturally occurring strengths and weaknesses. I always emphasize the importance of good effort and I encourage people to speak up if they need to take a break. I suggest that they may find the tests interesting and that I am interested in their feedback regarding the testing process. Finally, I reiterate that we will all meet again, usually the next week, for our follow-up appointment to review evaluation results and treatment recommendations.

In some circumstances, where I will not be meeting with the patient clinically to review results, such as an independent medical examination or a forensic case, I encourage patients to request a copy of the report through their attorney or claims manager. I write the report in plain English and in a respectful manner, regardless of my impressions and conclusions, so that my opinion and recommendations will be clear to the patient.

TEST SELECTION

Core Batteries: Key Areas of Function That Must Be Assessed

There is, of course, some difference of opinion among neuropsychologists regarding which tests to use. Some neuropsychologists have been trained with the Halstead Reitan neuropsychological assessment battery, whereas others have been taught the Luria–Nebraska approach or other process approaches.

Regardless of one's background, a core battery should assess the patient's premorbid intellectual level, current range of verbal and visual spatial problem-solving skills, attention and concentration, various aspects of memory, basic academic and linguistic skills, including naming and verbal fluency, and executive functions, such as planning, organizing, flexibility of thinking, trial-and-error reasoning, and ability to modify performance on the basis of feedback. Speed of thinking and performance needs to be gauged, along with at least some basic measures of fine motor function and sensory processing. Finally, assessment of personality variables are important for a full understanding of neuropsychological function. At the very least, some basic assessment of current mood is usually indicated.

My core clinical battery for adults (age 16–64) is extensive. Most of the patients I see are candidates for a comprehensive outpatient neuro-rehabilitation program, with a strong return-to-work emphasis. The majority have sustained traumatic brain injuries, and some form of litigation is likely. I want to see broad range of objective performance, with detailed information on many aspects of attention, memory, reasoning, effort, endurance, and coping style. My standard battery includes the following.

1. Wechsler Adult Intelligence Scale—III (WAIS-III)
2. Wechsler Memory Scale—Revised (WMS-R): Orientation and Mental Control, WMS-R Logical Memory I and II, Verbal Paired Associates I and II, Visual Reproduction I and II
3. Selective Reminding Test
4. Aphasia Screening Test
5. Boston Naming Test
6. Letter and animal fluency tests

7. Wide Range Achievement Test—Form 3
8. Trail Making Tests Parts A and B
9. Rey Osterrieth Complex Figure
10. Wisconsin Card Sorting Test
11. Halstead Category Test
12. Tactual Performance Test
13. Finger Tapping Test
14. Minnesota Multiphasic Personality Inventory—2 (short form) (MMPI-2) or MMPI–Adolescent Version
15. Rey 15 Item Test with Recall and Recognition Tests

Brief Batteries: Screening, Preliminary Review

For a brief screening review, I tend to use the Repeatable Brief Assessment of Neuropsychological Status (RBANS), in addition to a few supplementary items from the Cognistat, always with a good pretesting diagnostic interview. There are a number of good screening instruments available. I use this combination most often in an inpatient rehabilitation context, where patients are being screened for general areas of possible difficulty, or for patients with more profound impairments, e.g., advanced dementia.

Basic Batteries: Evaluations for Patients with Multiple Sclerosis, Brain Tumors, Early or Mild Dementias, and Stroke

For these groups of patients, I typically administer the following:

- Aphasia Screening Test
- Boston Naming Test
- Controlled Oral Word Association Test
- Animal Fluency Test
- Wide Range Achievement Test-3
- Wechsler Memory Scale-Revised: selected subtests:
  - Orientation
  - Mental Control
  - Logical Memory I and II
  - Visual Reproduction I and II
  - Verbal Paired Associates I and II
- Wechsler Adult Intelligence Scale–III
- Trails A and B
- Rey Osterrieth Complex Figure
- Wisconsin Card Sorting Test
- Finger Tapping
- MMPI-2 or Beck Depression Inventory

Extended Batteries: Rehabilitation Issues, Independent Medical Evaluations, and Legal Cases

For extended batteries, I typically combine the core battery with some of the selected additional testing items below. For example, I may increase task complexity, or I might use easier tasks, depending upon the clinical circumstance and the nature of my concerns. These additional tests may include any, although not all, of the following:

- Hiscock Digit Memory Test
- Paced Auditory Serial Addition Test
- Sensory Perceptual Examination
- Boston Diagnostic Aphasia Examination: Complex Ideational Material Subtest
- California Verbal Learning Test
- Rey Auditory Verbal Learning Test
- Benedict Visual Spatial Memory Test
- Gates MacGinitie Reading Comprehension Test
- Test of Reading Speed
- Lafayette Grooved Pegboard
- Fuld Object Memory Test
- Ruff Figural Fluency Test
- Porteus Mazes

SELECTIVE ADDITIONAL TESTING: AREAS OF CONCERN

Effort

Although I do not routinely give the Hiscock to every one of my clinical patients, in forensic cases or potential forensic cases (for instance, in the case of an independent medical exam [IME] or worker compensation), I always give a standardized measure of effort. In the clinical circumstance, I had sometimes given the Rey 15 Item Test, but I had concerns about its reliability and the interpretation of marginal scores. However, with the recent standardization and publication of a delayed recognition component to the Rey 15 Item, I now use it routinely with almost all of my clinical patients.

Premorbid IQ Estimates

Again, I do not routinely administer such measures in a purely clinical circumstance, but in potential forensic circumstances, I use the Wechsler Reading Achievement Test.

Significant Cognitive or Memory Impairment

For some clinical patients, memory impairment is so profound that a simpler memory test, such as the Fuld, is needed. It allows one to view list-learning performance without the stress of paragraphs or lengthier and solely auditory verbal learning tests. When only limited testing may be possible, the Fuld's set of concrete objects presented via multiple sensory modalities (tactile, visual, auditory), with extensive practice, fluency tasks, and recall and recognition trials, also provides a significant amount of useful information. It also has an alternate version, handy for later retesting.

Mild but Actual Neuropsychological Impairments

For other patients, deficits are so mild or subtle that more challenging measures of attention, memory, problem solving, and speed of thinking must be provided to determine if performance begins to break down under high demand conditions. Here, the PASAT or Selective Reminding Test, with their respective high speed and high volume/complexity requirements, can be useful sources of neuropsychological information.

Modified Batteries Secondary to Physical or Sensory Limitations

Patients with spinal cord injury, for example, who cannot manipulate objects or patients who have hearing or visual impairments may be testable in certain domains, but not in others. Standardized tests can still be selected and administered under proper conditions, but you will need to be both selective and creative. For example, motor free visual perceptual performances will be needed for the spinal cord patient, but all of the verbal auditory measures can be given. Alternatively, you may need to rely heavily upon visual tasks for a hearing-impaired patient but have a relatively easy time obtaining valid motor performances from them.

It is best to select standardized tests that fit the patient's physical capacities, rather than trying to modify test instructions or requirements. Modifications were not part of the original normative data and will render your obtained scores invalid.

There may always be the occasional unusual testing circumstance, when you may have no other way of eliciting cognitive behaviors of interest, unless you alter testing procedures. However, you need to remain fully cognizant that this does not generate a standardized score, and extreme caution in interpretation should be exercised and noted in your comments and written summaries.

EVALUATING PERSONALITY IN NEUROPSYCHOLOGICAL ASSESSMENT

It has been my experience that many neuropsychologists in clinical practice are not well trained in personality assessment. They may have basic psychometric knowledge of the MMPI and MMPI-2 (which I consider an essential tool), but they may not have had much exposure to the process of psychological evaluation during their graduate school or postdoctoral studies. Of perhaps equal importance, they have not had sufficient training in theories of personality development or function, other than the cognitive behavioral perspective, which is a useful but limited one. Many neuropsychologists have not spent much time directly involved in the process of psychotherapy, either as clinical trainees, licensed practitioners, or as patients.

If so, otherwise well-trained neuropsychologists may lack a full appreciation for the role of personality factors in cognitive disturbances, especially for some patients. These neuropsychologists may recognize basic affective problems like depression or anxiety. However, they may not be able to think critically about the potential interface between premorbid character structure, classic styles of personality strengths and vulnerabilities, as well as the conscious and unconscious factors in a patient's perception, motivation, information processing and behavior. Yet all of these factors are likely to affect the patient's clinical presentation, and in some cases, adversely affect their test scores. This may be so even when conscious effort is deemed to be valid, vis a vis performances on standardized measures of effort.

I consider the MMPI-2 results to be as important as IQ scores, memory performances, and other features of the strictly neuropsychological test protocol data in forming final opinions and recommendations for most patients between ages 16 and 65. When you are trying to distinguish the presence or absence of brain damage from normal performance, and yet remain open to the role of possible nonneurologic reasons for difficulty in function, you need to know as much as you possibly can about the psychological makeup of the patient.

You will strengthen your neuropsychological practice, the clinical usefulness of your reports, and the comprehensive value of your courtroom testimony if you obtain further training and supervision in the use of the MMPI and MMPI-2. While you are at it, consider added training or continuing education in other psychological areas, such as object relations theory, or case discussion of psychotherapy cases, even when brain injury or neurologic disease is not a comorbid problem. If you do this, you will be less vulnerable to misinterpreting cognitive difficulties as primarily or solely neurologically based, when, non-neurologic personality features and functional problems distort the patient's cognition.

CROSS CULTURAL ISSUES

An entire book could be written on this topic, but I am not the person to write that book. However, as a psychologist who values the appropriate use of standardized testing instruments, I ask you to consider the following: Unless a test was standardized on the population of people from which your patient comes, you are on very shaky neuropsychological ground when you interpret those test results.

In addition, the use of interpreters in a formal testing situation further complicates the potential threats to test score validity. There is truly no way to know for sure what the interpreter did or didn't say to the patient, even when everyone's intentions are beyond reproof. It is also possible that the meaning of the foreign word(s) into which a particular English word translates may inadvertently alter patients' chances for a correct answer to your specific questions.

If you are going to evaluate patients from a variety of cultural, ethnic, or linguistic groups, you will want to familiarize yourself with the literature on this topic and the various patient groups and to search out all available standardized instruments for those populations. Although some instruments are being restandardized with cross-cultural populations, there is still a general paucity of available comprehensive batteries. New instruments are also being developed to more fairly and accurately assess various non-English-speaking patients.

Please note I am not referring here to patients who are fully bilingual or who have obtained any significant portion of their higher education in English-speaking schools in the United States, Canada, or Great Britian. You should continue to exercise caution to be sure that these patients are from the same pool of Americans, Canadians, or some English-speaking people typically represented in the standardization samples for most of our tests. Further, one should always be cautious about interpreting subtests such as Picture Arrangement or other instruments that are heavily culturally based. Care must also be taken when reviewing tests where performance is dependent upon complex levels of verbal expression, reading, vocabulary, naming, or spelling knowledge in English, or upon everyday situations that are common for us, but not for people who are recent, or adult, immigrants.

I think it is still possible to derive clinically useful scores from testing an immigrant, depending entirely upon the tests that you are selecting. For example, mathematics tends to be a universal language, and paper-and-pencil measures of arithmetic skill should not be unduly affected. Single digit repetition is also a fairly universal task in Westernized countries or even in countries where telephones are a part of daily life. Nonverbal reasoning tasks that involve logic, appreciation of lines and angles, or ability to copy basic shapes are also likely to be useful in evaluation of patients from developed countries. Of course, you must exercise common sense and critical thinking in these circumstances, and always be cautious with your interpretation of results, stating those cautions clearly in your reports.

In the meantime, neuropsychologists are often asked to assist in answering diagnostic and treatment questions for a range of patients, from those who speak no English at all and are recent arrivals to this country to patients who spoke one language in the home as children but were English-educated in this country. Sometimes in a forensic or independent medical evaluation we are asked to answer those questions as well as we can. I encourage you to speak with your colleagues to determine how they handle this issue. There are strong and contradictory opinions on this topic about what is or is not advisable, fair, and helpful.

My preference is to refer these patients to practitioners who speak their language and have firsthand experience of the culture. However, because this is rarely an option, I take a cautiously pragmatic approach. I try to choose instruments in such circumstances that have the least cultural loading, I learn as much as possible about the patient's background and experience, I speak with the interpreter at length about some of his or her impressions of the patient's state of mind, and I elicit the interpreter's concerns. I follow my own testing advice.

USE OF PSYCHOMETRISTS

The use of psychometrists is another area of some controversy in the field of neuropsychological assessment. Some neuropsychologists, after they are trained and are in practice, perform little to none of their own testing, using psychometrists almost exclusively. Some practitioners do all of their own testing and have never used a psychometrist. During my postdoctoral fellowship, and in my first 6 years of full-time practice, I did all of my own testing. In a subsequent full-time job for 5 years, I typically saw the patient for a total of 2 hours, during which I completed the interview and some initial testing, then a well-trained psychometrist completed the testing per my instructions.

During my next phase of employment, for 6 years in my full-time private practice, I performed two to three evaluations per week, doing all of the testing for one patient, half of the testing for the second patient, and about a quarter of the testing for the occasional third patient. For the last 3 years of my practice, I have performed four full outpatient evaluations per week, with almost all of the formal testing done by two very experienced psychometrists. So I have had the opportunity to use no testing help, some help, and a lot of testing support. I can see advantages and disadvantages to each circumstance and a reasonable rationale for each.

I think there are several critical issues in deciding how to use psychometrists that mitigate the potential problems. The neuropsychologist needs to have first hand knowledge of all the tests to be administered and some direct experience giving them. Further, the neuropsychologist needs to conduct the in-depth interview with the patient and family and should not leave interviewing to the psychometrist. The psychometrists must also be well and thoroughly trained, not only in the specific tests but in the principles of valid test administration and scoring. Good patient care skills and the ability to write carefully detailed behavioral observations are also very important.

If everyone involved is appropriately trained and operating within the parameters of their specialty, I think any of the three basic approaches to testing is valid: Do all of your own testing, have a psychometrist do all of the testing, or do some of your own testing, with some help from a psychometrist.

There are trade-offs to any of these approaches. On the one hand, the psychologist may lose rich observational data if she or he is not present for all of the testing. Even though a good psychometrist will likely document all of the critical behaviors of interest, one cannot write down everything that transpires over a full day of testing. Some of the nuances of behavior are likely to be lost.

On the other hand, experienced psychometrists who regularly administer and score tests may be even more consistent in their testing and scoring then the neuropsychologist who has rarely done much of his or her own test administration. In this circumstance, the psychometrist is likely to yield more valid and reliable test data.

In some settings, or with some practice arrangements, the number of patients who needs to be seen for testing is quite high. When clinically important decisions rest in part on the results of timely evaluation, and there is only one neuropsychologist who cannot possibly do all of the testing alone, the use of psychometrists may be necessary for good patient care.

For example, a patient with relapsing–remitting multiple sclerosis who is receiving a disease-modifying therapy may note significant decline in his or her thinking over a 6-month period, but present no further physical changes and only marginal change on MRI. The physician needs to know relatively soon how this person's neuropsychological test scores compare to baseline, to determine if neurologically based change appears to be the cause, and to decide if a different disease-modifying drug treatment is warranted. If the psychologist by him- or herself was able to see only a few people a week, the resulting wait for evaluation is not likely to be tenable.

REPORT FORMATS

I like to be able to glance at the first page of a report, and quickly see the patient's age, education, occupation, marital status, handedness, date of injury or onset of illness, date of testing, the referral source, the neuropsychologist's name, and the date of the final report. (See Appendix A for a copy of my typical report format.) I place all of this information in my first subheading, Identifying Information.

Next, I want to know all of the relevant medical background, presented in concise form. This includes the type of injury or illness, basic findings of MRI and computed tomography (CT) scans, any other injuries or complications the patient may have suffered and, briefly, any relevant premorbid problems. If the patient spent an extensive amount of time in the hospital, or on inpatient rehabilitation or at a skilled nursing facility as part of recovery, I like to see those dates or lengths of stay. The specific reasons for referral should be clearly stated.

I find it helpful to include a brief section on evaluation procedures, so I can convey what was done, when, and by whom. I also like to note what records or collateral information were available to me at the time of testing and report preparation, for example, whether I spoke to family members, an employer, or if detailed records arrive late.

I include a fairly detailed section on the interview and relevant personal and social history for two reasons. 1) It provides a more complete picture of the patient as a fully realized human being, with longstanding strengths and coping abilities or limitations, in a larger life context. 2) Most of the patients I see are going to be admitted to an outpatient neurorehabilitation program. In that therapeutic context, a thorough psychosocial history is extremely helpful for all treating staff.

There are some important exceptions to including a detailed psychosocial history in a neuropsychological report. If I were providing a report for a 16 year old returning to school after a TBI, I would not detail so many aspects of personal history for two reasons: One is to protect the adolescent's privacy when that information may not be relevant or could be damaging. I may keep that information in mind when I make treatment recommendations, but not everyone needs to know the personal historical information in detail. Second, I want to maximize focus on the residual cognitive and neurobehavioral problems related to the student's injury or illness, so a full appreciation of neurologically based problems is emphasized and treated.

In a separate section on behavioral observations I detail the patient's approach to testing, his or her degree of positive or negative involvement, and his or her reaction to the testing. I might include comments on the patient's responses to various test items. The emphasis in the behavioral observations section is to capture the physical, affective, and behavioral flavor of this unique individual, as knowledge of these facts can guide us in drawing conclusions from the test results. This section can also include review of items I would see in a basic mental status exam report (such as affect, rate of speech, eye contact, demeanor, and appearance). It also includes an emphasis on the process features of patient performance, e.g., how they approached various tasks or reacted to failures.

Next, I itemize Specific Tests Administered, in a list or column form, rather than as a paragraph. It is much easier to scan through the list of tests if they are laid out on separate lines, rather than as part of a narrative.

For my summary of examination findings, I lead off with a paragraph or two, summarizing the patient's key findings, areas of difficulty, areas of ability, and how these are or are not consistent with the medical history. Then I detail more specific scores in the body of the report, starting with IQ performances. Where appropriate, I also indicate some combination of percentile ranks or comments on the mild, moderate, or severe nature of possible impairments in the areas of memory, language, academic skills, attention and concentration, speed of thinking, executive skills, and personality findings.

My diagnostic impression section is a very brief summary or restatement of the above, so referring physicians and others can turn to this section, read my final conclusions, and then see the recommendations section immediately following.

I encourage you to ask colleagues for copies of their report formats and to choose what makes the most sense for you in your practice. You may modify your report format over time or depending upon the testing situation. Forensic circumstances may require a greater detailing of medical records reviewed; other testing circumstances, such as a brief evaluation of a geriatric patient may not require much information in the examination procedures sections.

REVIEW OF TEST RESULTS

On the day I interview patients as part of their evaluations, I also schedule a 1-hour follow-up appointment to be held the following week with them and their family member(s). At that follow-up meeting, I review test results, recommendations, and I may clarify a point or two with them that I want to revisit, in light of their test performance. For example, the psychometrist may have noted that the patient was mentioning shoulder pain on one side when completing the Tactual Performance Test (TPT). This may have affected time to completion on a particular trial of the TPT, yet there may have been nothing in the records to suggest shoulder problems. After this meeting with the patient and family, I dictate my final report and recommendations.

In Forensic cases or IMEs, I review all of the records one final time and I complete the report, sending copies to the attorneys or to the worker compensation carrier, but I do not send copies of the report directly to the patient. I also explain to the patient that the report will be going to the referral source, and how the patient may obtain a copy.

Finally, I would like to re-emphasize one point: Reports should be written in plain English so they are understandable to the referral source and to the patient. In addition, even when you are not planning to give a copy of the report to the patient, the report still should be written in such a way that a reasonable person would not be insulted by the tone of your descriptions and findings. It is important to be as honest and as respectful as possible. Imagine someone has tested you and is describing your areas of strength, vulnerability, and behavior, for publication and perusal by other individuals. Let that guide you in choosing the language of your reports.

DICTATION VERSUS TYPING IT YOURSELF

I have one word of advice here: Dictate!

It will take you at least three times as long—if you type quickly—to type a report as it does to dictate a report. Although report templates may help, so you don't need to type the list of tests or headings, for each new patient, typing is not an efficient use of your time.

Let me suggest the following for those of you still typing, who like to think as you write, and who feel you function much more effectively in the written rather than the spoken domain. There are some preliminary steps to prepare for effective dictation:

1. Follow a well-organized outline in your interview of the patient.
2. When you are reviewing medical records, make yourself an outline or brief chronological list of the relevant facts and have this at your side when you are ready to dictate the report.
3. Have a well-organized data summary sheet for your test results, set up in a format that flows with the Summary of Examination Findings section of your report.
4. Make a detailed outline to follow in dictating. This will likely be your report format, but with the suboutlines of medical data and patient history available as content guides.
5. Clear your desk of all other materials, except for this patient's records and test results, and your outline formats.
6. Organize all of your testing protocols in the file in the order in which you will generally be addressing them, so that if you need to double-check something, you can quickly turn to that protocol, rather than randomly search your file.
7. If you are using a telephone dictation system, have the cue card in front of you (e.g., "Press 4 to pause, press 2 to dictate, press 3 to rewind") to prevent inadvertent errors.
8. Have your secretary or transcriptionist email you the report as an attachment. It is much faster to review a report already typed and make

modifications, then to sit in front of your computer, lost in thought, distracted or overly involved by questions of word usage. Get it done as efficiently and accurately as you can.

9. Your schedule needs to protect dictation times so you will be uninterrupted. It is not efficient to begin to dictate, be interrupted midstream, and then try to come back to it later.

DISSEMINATION OF REPORTS

In general, the referring person, the patient, and you should have copies of the report. Always check that you and the patient have the same understanding as to who will or will not receive copies of the report. Make sure the patient understands the limits and protections of confidentiality in his or her particular testing circumstance.

PRESERVATION OF TESTING FILES AND RAW DATA

I save all testing data for 10 years. As a contract employee at various agencies, I have noticed that institutional policies for data preservation vary from 5 to 10 years. It can be especially critical to preserve test data for a much longer term for children or adolescents who have been injured or ill, and for whom future comparisons will be essential. I routinely evaluate patients who are now in their 20s or 30s and who sustained very severe injuries or tumors as children. It has been invaluable to see their early records to fully appreciate their current difficulties or strengths I now see.

EXERCISES

What is your core battery of tests?

Why?

Will you plan to use psychometrists?

Why or why not?

Gather examples of report templates from colleagues or supervisors, and decide upon your own format.

Estimate how much time it will take you to prepare reports. If you are just getting started in your practice, multiply that estimate by 2.7 and plan for the higher number of hours.

11

TREATMENT PRACTICES FOR NEUROPSYCHOLOGISTS

Qualified neuropsychologists tend to fall within two broad groups vis à vis the focus or emphasis of their early training. In my opinion, these two groups are equally well trained, but with much different clinical strengths. Their respective graduates need to appreciate and ultimately address their own training strengths and weaknesses when designing a private practice. This training emphasis will have major implications for the types of patients each neuropsychologist group can competently treat, unless further training is obtained.

YOUR TRAINING BACKGROUND AND FUTURE TRAINING NEEDS

One group of neuropsychologists has usually attended APA-approved clinical psychology graduate programs followed by internships that include neuropsychology rotations. They then complete formal postdoctoral fellowships in neuropsychology. This group generally has had ongoing training in psychotherapy with outpatient psychiatric populations as part of graduate school and internship experience.

The other group of neuropsychologists has attended neuropsychology doctoral programs and completed internships with a neuropsychology or rehabilitation emphasis. These graduates tend to accumulate their postdoctoral hours in neuropsychology and/or rehabilitation settings. Their training as therapists tends to be focused upon neurologic populations, with an emphasis upon cognitive and neurobehavioral changes related to disease or injury. They have little or no training in clinical psychology.

Long term, it generally benefits neuropsychologists from the first group to expand and deepen their specific neuropsychological knowledge. This group has usually received good grounding in the basics of neuroanatomy, neuropathology, the nature and impact of various neurologic diseases, as well as good psychometric training. However, they have typically not had the level of formal classroom reading and discussion in focused areas of neuropsychological interest that provides that last piece of precision and expertise.

Practitioners from the second group often need to have more training and practice as effective psychotherapists. For this group, ongoing consultation and supervision in psychotherapy, object relations, and psychodynamic theory and practice will be important for a more sophisticated understanding of human behavior. This group often needs some degree of continuing clinical consultation to learn how to function more comfortably and wisely as psychologists, and to develop a degree of comfort with the emotional issues and reactions of their patients.

WHAT KIND OF PRACTICE DO YOU WANT?

Depending upon the nature of your own training, you can craft a treatment practice that allows you to make the most effective use of your strengths, while minimizing areas of potential limitations in your training. Especially when you are beginning independent practice limiting yourself to treating patients with whom you are competent is a critical first step. You are more likely to be effective with these patients than a patients for whom you are not yet adequately prepared.

Of course, some practitioners combine a clinical psychology practice with a neuropsychology practice. They may spend part of their time providing individual psychotherapy to psychiatric and brain-injured outpatients, while they devote the other part of their clinical time to conducting neuropsychological evaluations.

Other practitioners may spend most of their clinical time in an evaluation practice, while providing some outpatient psychotherapy with a strong cognitive rehabilitation emphasis, or they may see only brain-injured patients and their families to provide support, education, and oversight of neurobehavioral problems and strategy development.

OTHER PARTS OF GOOD CLINICAL PRACTICE DEVELOPMENT

Good practice development includes knowing which patients you can best serve and educating potential referral sources about the patients you can help them manage. It also includes finding your own set of reliable colleagues to whom you can refer patients you prefer not to treat.

One excellent way to establish a neuropsychologically based outpatient psychotherapy practice is to form relationships with both inpatient rehabilitation teams and with formal outpatient neurorehabilitation programs. These institutionally based programs are usually prepared to deliver intensive treatment over a relatively brief period—usually a few weeks of inpatient rehabilitation, a few months in outpatient programs. However, they may have a surfeit of patients. If so, they may not be able to provide more long-term support and intervention, which many seriously brain-injured individuals require to function well in the community, and they will welcome additional clinical resources.

ESTABLISHING SHORT-TERM AND LONG-TERM GROUPS

Many institutions also are not able to provide long-term family education and support groups for the relatives of brain-injured patients. You could fill this need by offering patient education groups, for which you charge a nominal fee—perhaps $60 for 4 weeks of 90 min weekly groups. You may also provide a quarterly, 6-month, or yearly syllabus with various topics or speakers organized into 1-month modules. If you publish your syllabus 6 months to a year in advance, families can select the month or months they wish to attend and can register in advance.

The fees are really a form of tuition that people pay at the time of registration. You can decide upon your own policy for cancellation and reimbursement. I follow a policy similar to that employed by institutions of higher learning, i.e., you may cancel your registration with some advance notice and receive your tuition back. Once you have attended the class and have received the extensive notebook of handouts, tuition is not refundable. You should also determine the minimum number of registrants you need to make the class financially sound. Then as part of the registration packet, you can let people know in advance that a given module will only meet if there are, for example, 10 paid registrants.

You can also create a roster of guest speakers from other colleagues in your private practice community, be they physicians, physical therapists, speech pathologists, etc, The family education and support group can be organized so you have a guest speaker on a topic of interest for the first 30 minutes, then a break with coffee and questions, and then 45 minutes for general discussion and support.

These groups can be advertised to the community at large or with your patient's prior knowledge and permission to contact family members, only to the families of your own past and present patients.

You can also develop your own long-term outpatient support group for brain-injured patients. It might meet once a month for 1½–2 hours to discuss concerns and issues. You need to perform brief initial screening interviews with patients to determine if they are appropriate candidates for the group. It is helpful to know what other sources of individual therapy support they have, if they are not your patients, to insure their well-being. You will also need the patient's permission to communicate with their primary therapist.

INDIVIDUAL TREATMENT IN A NEUROPSYCHOLOGY PRACTICE

Appropriately trained neuropsychologists have the option of providing two different kinds of therapy services. One is traditional psychotherapy for patients with brain injury. Here the focus of treatment is on emotional and psychological problems, such as changes in the sense of self, depression, anxiety, and the patient's attempts to establish a sense of normalcy and meaning in life after brain injury.

The other individual treatment falls within the domain of cognitive rehabilitation, with interventions specifically designed to address residual changes in thinking and acquired (that is, neurologic) behavior problems. Although there is overlap between these two therapies since they address neurobehavioral changes that trouble the patient, there are also some clear differences in emphasis of the intervention.

Within cognitive rehabilitation treatment for patients with brain damage, the primary treatment emphasis is typically upon new problems in thinking or behavior that form barriers to adaptive function that are a result of the patient's brain injury or illness. For example, your treatment may emphasize strategies for increased awareness of deficits, such as impulsivity or poor judgment, as well as specific strategies to manage those deficits more effectively. These may be practiced both within and after the session.

Or, the patient may have significant problems with memory that are adversely affecting his or her function and the impact on other people. The treatment might emphasize such specific behavioral solutions as use of a weekly planner, good note-taking strategies, ways to improve attention, methods for asking questions of the speaker, options for slowing down the speaker if information is being presented too fast to be absorbed by the patient, writing of summary notes, or establishing times of day to refer to one's notes. This is usually practiced within the session.

BILLING AND REIMBURSEMENT ISSUES

There was good news in the year 2002 for neuropsychologists who provide treatment services. An expanded list of Current Procedural Terminology, (CPT) codes became available. (See Appendix I for a list of these codes.) These codes allow psychologists to bill under a medical diagnosis and to charge for the actual cognitive rehabilitation treatments they have long provided (see previous clinical examples). This treatment can include addressing patients' difficulties with attention, memory, problem solving, planning, and organization. Treatment and training in compensatory techniques for neurologically based changes in thinking no longer requires an inappropriate mental health diagnosis. This charge will be reimbursed as part of the patient's medical benefit which is ordinarily better than the mental health benefit.

Psychotherapy should still be billed when appropriate under the individual (90801 for diagnostic interview, 90806 for an hour of psychotherapy) and group mental health codes as appropriate. This is typically done with a mental health condition noted as the primary diagnosis and the secondary diagnosis is the medical condition.

OTHER PRACTICE OPTIONS: EMPLOYEE ASSISTANCE PROGRAM CONTRACTS

You may wish to contact the personnel departments at companies in your community to learn more about their employee assistance programs. Large companies typically arrange off-site or community treatment options for their employees. It is a good opportunity to educate employers about common neurologically based problems that may present on the job, such as residual effects of head injury or stroke. You can discuss with employers what evaluation and treatment services you offer. The company may create a contract with you, so you can bill them directly for your services to their employees. In these situations, payment is typically prompt. This population of patients can often benefit from your clear advice and support regarding their residual problems, especially as these affect work performance.

OTHER PRACTICE OPTIONS: CASE MANAGEMENT SERVICES

Another option for neuropsychologists is to function as long-term case managers, or as a primary consultant to case managers who are trying to orchestrate and direct the daily care of severely brain-injured patients. These patients typically have long-term trusts or settlements that provide for their lifelong needs and usually have significant cognitive, physical, and/or behavioral limitations that require continued intervention. Both the patient and his or her treating staff members benefit from periodic review of treatment plans or troubleshooting of behavioral problems. Sometimes these are problems that have resurfaced, that are proving intractable, or that may threaten the person's chances to remain in a supported home environment. Although you may not be providing direct treatment, you can provide consultation to the patient, the family, the case manager, and the home or group home staff, and your fees will be paid by the trust.

EXERCISES

For what types of treatment services are you currently qualified?

What portion of your practice is likely to be psychotherapy-based, and what portion is likely to be cognitive-rehabilitation based?

Where are patients with these needs likely to be found in your community? Do you prefer a combination of individual and group treatments?

Would you prefer a family education and consultation practice?

How can you offer your services to these patients, both directly and through their primary referring providers?

12

NUTS AND BOLTS OF YOUR EVALUATION PRACTICE

Let's review the method for developing your neuropsychological evaluation practice, from initial referral to timetables for completion of reports and billing.

REFERRALS

Referral Etiquette

Always thank your referral sources for each patient referred for evaluation or treatment. One efficient approach is to send a letter thanking them for each referral, and also let them know when the patient is scheduled to be seen. When you have completed the evaluation, call the provider to discuss the findings and any further treatment recommendations. Ask how they prefer to receive your feedback. For instance, do they prefer to receive the written report prior to any further discussion? At what point would they like to talk with you, if at all?

Part of good referral etiquette is to remain available by phone. Some specific suggestions:

1. Always return your telephone calls and voicemail messages as soon as possible during your work week. If you don't have time to talk at length, call anyway or have your secretary call, and arrange a time when you can speak further. If you are calling a provider, offer your pager number and blocks of time when you can call back. If you are calling a potential patient, offer some telephone appointment times when you will be available to talk to them by telephone.

2. If there are specific times or days during the week that you know you will not be available, say so on your office voice mail. (For instance, "Calls received after 4 P.M. on Thursdays may not be returned until the following Monday.")

3. Reserve time in your daily schedule to return or receive calls, and make these times known.

4. In the process of returning calls from patients who are interested in neuropsychological evaluation, you may discover that the patient has been evaluated previously by another psychologist. It is appropriate to ask why the patient is not returning to that psychologist for retesting. It is also helpful to obtain (a) a copy of the prior evaluation report and (b) the patient's permission to speak with the prior neuropsychologist. If a patient refuses permission to speak to current or previous clinicians, this may signal trouble. I am usually not willing to see the patient in this circumstance.

5. If you have any reason to be concerned about the referral, don't agree to see the patient until your concerns have been satisfied. In general, I accept only professionally generated referrals. If patients contact me, I encourage them to obtain a referral for testing from their primary care physician or neurologist. This may also be required for insurance reimbursement on some health plans.

EDUCATING REFERRAL SOURCES

It may take new referral sources time to learn which kinds of patients you prefer to see. They may also need to learn the kinds of referral questions that can be addressed via neuropsychological assessment. You can offer to attend departmental or group practice meetings and discuss the benefits and limitations of neuropsychological assessment. Be aware of the kinds of patients the attendees typically see.

Provide a list of guidelines for referral, so colleagues have something tangible to review (see Appendix). When you speak to groups, such as self-insured companies, take these guideline and other information you have developed on other topics of local interest. Join and then educate organizations such as a local Providers in Workers' Compensation group (see Appendix B).

Consider setting up a website that describes your work so people can browse your menu of services, fees, philosophy, and affiliations. Your website can be an effective way to conserve time and resources, as well as be a means for people to easily contact you, serving as both a point of information and point of contact for you.

PURPOSE OF TESTING

Be sure you understand what is expected when testing is requested. Be sure that neuropsychological assessment is actually the appropriate first step. For example, if patients with known or suspected neurological disease or injury have not had a recent medical examination, you will want to suggest they have an update prior to seeing you. Everyone involved in the referral and testing process should have a similar understanding and expectation regarding the purpose of the evaluation and the use to which the results will be put. It is also important that both referrers and patients understand what questions can't be answered by testing. (See Appendix B.)

For example, I may conclude that a brain-injured man has the requisite intellectual abilities to handle college-level coursework. So I can answer the question, "Is he capable of college-level work?" But that answer doesn't also guarantee graduation from college or predict successful employment. There are usually additional factors that must be satisfactorily addressed to predict the likelihood of life achievement. Additionally, referrers and patients need to understand that performance on neuropsychological variables is only one important element of evaluation and treatment. As part of your recommendations, it is also helpful if you can outline the specific types of support or treatment interventions that would maximize the patient's positive long-term outcome.

Working Diagnosis

Insurance companies often want at least a tentative diagnosis prior to authorizing neuropsychological evaluations. In most instances, this may be a relatively straightforward matter (for instance, history of possible concussion or traumatic brain injury, multiple sclerosis, stroke or anoxic injury). (See Appendix H for common diagnoses list.)

In some cases where the diagnosis is less clear, but where there is reason to suspect brain-based changes in function, I use a more general ICD-9 International Statistical Classification of Diseases Ninth Rev. category. I avoid the use of psychiatric diagnoses unless, of course, that is the primary reason for referral. Otherwise, one of the medical diagnosis codes should be used. (See Appendix H for ICD-9 codes.)

Scheduling of Patients for Interview and Testing

My typical neuropsychological evaluation requires a full-day appointment. This usually begins at 8:30 when I greet the patient and family in the waiting room and escort them to the office where the interview with me will be held. When the interview is completed, usually by 9:30 or 10 A.M., depending upon the patient, family, the complexity of the history or slowness of function, I take them to the testing area. I give them a brief break while I meet with the psychometrist. I review with the psychometrist concerns or impressions regarding the patient that I think could potentially affect test validity or the testing process, and I select the lists of tests to be administered.

I then introduce the patient and family member to the psychometrist and leave them to work out the days' breaks and lunchtime. Breaks at midmorning and midafternoon, along with an hour for lunch, are our typical pace, with modifications available as needed. Formal testing is typically completed by 4:30 P.M. That does not include my time reviewing medical records, nor the psychometrists' scoring time or time spent writing behavioral observations. In my current practice, with the luxury of two psychometrists, they always double check each other's scoring, and the completed files are returned to me in 2–3 working days time.

Sometimes, the patient isn't able to finish in one day and must return to complete testing. If we know in advance that they are likely to need extra time to complete the test battery, we schedule accordingly.

Time Frame for Report

I typically dictate a brief, initial summary note of test findings as part of my review of results held with the patient the week following completion of testing. This note details the primary strengths and problem areas, the diagnostic impression, and treatment recommendations. In clinical cases, copies of this note are always sent to the referring physician, to the patient and to my file.

The final report should be completed within 1 to 2 weeks after testing. Delays do occur, if you discover at the time of testing that additional records must be obtained, or collateral interviews completed. In general, it is good practice to require a full set of medical and pertinent academic or work records prior to scheduling the evaluation appointment.

Some of my colleagues in private practice routinely take several weeks to complete complex cases, but their referral sources are kept informed of patient progress and preliminary findings prior to receiving the final report. You need to determine what is appropriate and acceptable for the people who are referring patients for evaluation.

For example, the division of vocational rehabilitation may not be able to implement any treatment or return-to-work recommendations until the counselor has received your complete report. However, in forensic circumstances, you may be awaiting the receipt of medical records, school records, or prior test data from another examiner, and this may necessarily delay completion of Independent Medical Exam (IME) or legal reports.

MECHANISMS OF FEEDBACK TO REFERRAL SOURCES AND PATIENTS

I use three general mechanisms of feedback to providers and two for my patients:

Provider Feedback

1. If a provider in my department has referred a patient for testing, I usually offer informal feedback at our subsequent weekly panel meeting. Those providers also have easy access to the electronic record and can simply look up a copy of the patient follow-up note and the report. I also make sure these providers are on my list of dictated report recipients.
2. For faculty providers in other departments of the University of Washington Medical Center (UWMC), I try to send a quick email note, using the patient's first name, first initial of their last name, and patient registration number. I also copy the providers on my dictation. I don't typically call these faculty providers because they are often difficult to reach directly and because it is relatively easy for them to contact me if they have further questions after seeing my e-mail note.
3. For providers who are outside the UWMC system, I try to arrange to speak to him or her in person. If I know that she or he prefers to be interrupted for this feedback, I ask the nurse or secretary to do so. If this is not possible, I will leave a message regarding the basic findings and recommendations, what may be needed from the primary care physician, and how I may best be reached. I also include my pager number, so I can return calls immediately when possible.

The referring provider is always copied on dictation of follow-up visits as well as the final reports. I may also request that the provider initiate and FAX a referral for treatment, such as individual cognitive rehabilitation via speech, or other appropriate services for the patient. If I am recommending the patient be seen by therapists near their home community, I try to provide the names of therapists in that area to the patient as well as to his or her referring physician.

Feedback to Patients

As the initial interview is drawing to a close, I try to schedule a follow-up appointment to review test results.

Some of my patients travel long distances for their evaluations and are either not able to remain in the area long enough for me to provide their testing results to them, or they might not have another return visit scheduled for several months. If a timely in-person follow-up visit is not feasible, I arrange a phone appointment. While this is not my preference for discussing findings, it can work well nonetheless.

Estimated Costs of Evaluation

We always estimate for patients the probable cost of the evaluation. We also explain that even if insurance companies have authorized the service, there is no guarantee that the fees will actually be paid. We strongly encourage patients to speak directly to their insurance companies to learn the details of their policy. We tell patients the hospital charges for a psychologist's and a psychometrist's time. We try to avoid unpleasant surprises when the bill is received.

My full evaluations typically include 7–8 hours of psychometrist time and 4–5 hours of my own. The total 11–13 hours is an approximate figure that we provide to patients, providers (if requested), and to the insurance companies. The fee schedule at UWMC (2003) is set at about $155 per hour for my time and $115 per hour for testing by the psychometrists. Typical total bills are about $1,695.

Patient Information Handouts and Registration Forms

Regardless of work setting, I always make sure that patients are provided with a confirmation letter for their appointments and directions for driving and parking. I also make sure they know what to expect for the day: it is eight hours; they will meet initially with me first and then the psychometrist; the patient should bring their spouse or primary family member for the interview; there will be a lunch break and other breaks; they are reminded to bring reading glasses if needed; to arrange for transportation.

In my private practice, I also require that a basic information sheet be completed prior to scheduling an appointment. I typically send a packet of forms to the patient, and ask them to read, complete, and sign those prior to scheduling an evaluation appointment and to return the forms with a deposit to reserve their testing date (see Appendix C). Half of the estimated cost of testing is due at the time of evaluation, and the other half due within 30 days of the final billing.

I also make clear that it is the patient's responsibility to obtain pre-authorization of services. Of course I provide an insurance-appropriate invoice, but I do not pursue payment from insurance companies. I spent the first year of my 6 initial years of private practice chasing payments from insurance companies, after which I decided it was a waste of my time, and thus, a significant indirect cost to me. The only exceptions to the 50% down, 50% within 30 days of billing are (a) worker compensation referrals, (b) contract work where I am paid directly for my time by an institution or company and do not need to submit a separate billing, (c) legal work which is paid in advance, or (d) work for the Division of Vocational Rehabilitation. In the last instance, authorization vouchers are provided before I see the patient and payment is generally prompt.

Obtaining Records

What Are Pertinent Records

Depending on the referral questions, you may need the following:

Emergency room reports
Hospital admission and discharge summaries
Outpatient evaluation and treatment notes
Narrative reports of MRI, CT, EEG, and evoked potentials
Ambulance or aide car reports
Police reports
Pictures of the damaged automobile (if applicable)
Outpatient physician notes relevant to diagnosis or referral questions
School records including transcripts and achievement test scores
Treatment records
Prior testing reports and protocols
Work performance evaluations

Not every patient will need all of the above. However, in every setting, it is vital to have records that document the reason for referral and past relevant medical history. Some practitioners will not schedule a patient for an evaluation appointment until relevant records are received.

When you are first establishing your private practice, you may not be able to afford to pay someone else to help you with record collection. Fortunately, it is easy to modify certain requirements, such as all records in advance, that might function as hurdles to accessing your services when you are building your practice. Ask the referring provider's office for records and let them know that you will be delighted to see the patient, and that you will need the records before the testing date. After you contact the patient and schedule the appointment, call the provider's office to let them know the date by which the records are needed. Set up a tickler file to remind you to check well in advance of the testing appointment, to make sure you have all of the information you need. There have certainly been occasions where the patients arrived to be seen before their records did. In those circumstances, I let the patient know I will need to see all of their records before I finalize their report.

Once you see the patient, you may discover other records that would be helpful. But you need to have the basic medical history, and any prior relevant testing before completing your evaluation report.

Release of Information for Additional Information

During my interview with the patient and family, I may discover I need additional information, and I obtain the patient's permission to obtain those records. For instance, I may need a college transcript that the patient will request be sent to me. Other times, the patient will sign a release that allows me to contact hospitals or doctors in other states to obtain additional prior records. Sometimes I discover that the patient has been previously tested as part of a Social Security evaluation, and I obtain permission to request the test results.

In some circumstances, I will need the patient's permission to speak to a family member who was not able to be present for the interview. I may also request permission to speak to an employer. This is not to convey information at this preliminary stage but to obtain, for instance, more direct information on current job performance and observed strengths and problems.

INSURANCE PREAUTHORIZATION OF SERVICES

Private Insurance

I have learned a lot in the last 3 years of institutional life about effective preauthorization of neuropsychological services. When I became Director of the Neuropsychology Testing Lab in my department I needed to improve clinical volumes, billing, and collections. I had to deal with a vast range of insurance plans and insurance decision rules. I wanted, of course, to make sure that the lab succeeded, both clinically and fiscally, and that my psychometrists could count on job security. I also knew that with improved revenues came increased negotiating power and independence as a psychologist in this medical setting.

There were no support staff assigned to the lab and no one to provide preauthorization help when I arrived. I negotiated with the two psychometrists, who obviously know a lot about testing, to begin arranging the preauthorization approvals. They were far more effective in explaining to insurance personnel why testing was needed than was the typical office assistant. The psychometrists also understood the implications of a particular medical diagnosis and could explain to a naïve claims manager, for example, why a patient with multiple sclerosis might need a neuropsychological evaluation. It saved me precious clinical time, facilitated a steady flow of paid evaluations, and kept overhead costs down. When difficult economic times swept through the medical center, our lab was spared cutbacks and closure, in large part because we had kept our overhead so low, and we maximized our reimbursement.

All or part of this model of operation are appropriate and useful to private practice, and I recommend the following:

1. Educate patients so they understand they are ultimately responsible for payment of the evaluation; have them sign an agreement and provide a 50% deposit. This will at least cover your basic costs.
2. Offer to provide preauthorization advice as a way to help maximize insurance coverage.
3. If you develop a large evaluation practice—4 full evaluations per week—you may decide to pay your psychometrists to do the preauthorization. They can't test 8 hours a day, every day and maintain their sanity, and arranging the preauthorization allows you to help patients and maximize the likelihood of appropriate payment.
4. Use only the applicable medical diagnosis and the 96117 code for neuropsychological assessment preauthorization and billing.
5. Do not use any psychiatric CPT codes or psychiatric ICD-9 codes in the billing or preauthorization (unless, of course, those are the ones that properly apply).
6. Do not become a Medicare or Medicaid provider. Medicare may seem to provide a reasonable level of reimbursement. However, it does not, in my opinion, because of the legal risks you incur, the confusing and sometimes contradictory requirements that constitute compliance, and the arbitrary rules and limitations imposed on every area of your practice if you are a provider. I would prefer to accept no insurance and charge a meager fee rather than deal with Medicaid and Medicare as a private practitioner.

Additionally, you should appreciate that you have no leverage with any insurance company. You are not their paying customer. They are trying, of course, to maximize profits. It is not in their financial best interest to expedite payment of your bills. They are earning interest on that money while you are waiting for it. To the extent that any insurance company wishes to maintain or improve its enrollment of patients in particular health plans, or to avoid bad press because of patient dissatisfactions, their customer (your patient) does potentially have some leverage. The company needs to be reasonably responsive to their own paying customers. If patients register enough complaints about poor service, either individually or through their employers, or if large private practice groups of physicians decide that they can no longer afford to see patients with particular types of coverage, insurance systems may change in response. But they won't change in response to your calls.

Contract Services and Legal Work

If you have initial agreements with insurers, such as your state workers' compensation carrier, or the Division of Vocational Rehabilitation, and a written guarantee of payment, it is fine to schedule and see the patient, and to expect payment for your approved services. For some attorneys with a proven record of timely payment, it is probably also fine to see their clients and bill when you have completed the evaluation. Initially, however I would require full advance payment. Establish a fee that you think will cover your record review and all evaluation and report time.

As I've discussed in previous chapters, developing contractual relationships with local hospitals or medical centers is a good supplement to any private practice, especially a newly established one. In these contract relationships, you will be paid a an hourly rate for your part-time services. If you have negotiated a minimum weekly number of hours for guaranteed payment, your employer has strong incentive to keep the patient flow moving towards you, and it saves you from wasted, unpaid time that you had otherwise reserved for their patients.

TIMELY BILLING AND COLLECTIONS

In the institutional setting, bills typically need to be submitted as soon as the patient's testing is completed. I know from experience that it takes me 2–3 hours to prepare a standard report, and I add that time to the hours I have already spent in initial record review, interview time with the patient and others, and any discussion time with the referral source. The 2–3 hours for report preparation includes a review of my summary notes from the patient's medical and other records, the patient and family interview notes, all of the test data, my time to interpret the MMPI-2, time to dictate the report, and time in final review and edit of the completed report. I am fairly efficient after more than 20 years in practice. It may take an inexperienced neuropsychologist longer to do report preparation, and you should bill accordingly.

In my private practice, I usually did not submit the bill until the report was completed. This provided me with a good incentive for relatively rapid report completion. However, always submit your bill within 30 days of your patient's completion of testing.

The challenge of collections with neuropsychological evaluations is threefold:

1. You do not typically have an ongoing therapeutic relationship with the patient, which presumably would provide them with an added incentive to pay you and maintain a positive connection.

2. The bill is for a large amount of money, which can be overwhelming for most people who do not have an extra $1,800 available to them.

3. The patient may not like your conclusions or be unhappy that the insurance company is not paying as much as the patient had expected.

For all of these reasons, I try to avoid being in the business of collections. I protect myself from this by knowing what insurance companies generally pay, making sure I have medical referral for the testing, and collecting a large deposit from the patient prior to testing.

Most of my private evaluation patients paid their bills, but a few required me to generate repeated calls and letters. They eventually paid, but the process was irritating and costly. You may need to be stiffed one time by a patient you were confident would pay you before you modify your billing and collections practices. I recommend advance payment that will cover your costs.

EXERCISES

1. *How do I want to educate referral sources and patients about the nature of neuropsychological assessment?*
2. *How do I want to formally thank referral sources? By separate letter or by my report?*
3. *Who will do insurance preauthorization for my testing patients?*
4. *How do I want to bill and collect for my work?*
5. *How do I want to design my testing schedule (e.g., all-day evaluation appoinments or two partial days)?*

13

HOW TO DESIGN AND IMPLEMENT A COGNITIVE GROUP

INTRODUCTION

There are many different kinds of treatment groups that neuropsychologists may develop. Some groups emphasize ways to manage changes in thinking; other groups may focus on emotions and coping. Some practitioners offer a series of continuing groups that target particular skills, such as memory compensatory techniques or social skills. Other groups provide support for family members. Some groups function as a form of continuing education for patients and their families, with invited speakers, course notebooks, and even weekly assignments or homework to enrich the discussion.

The full range and particulars of those myriad groups, such as knowledge of group process, training and selection of the therapists, patient recruitment, ideal mix and screening of group members, development of content and handouts, probably constitutes a separate book. However, in the closing chapter of this book, I want to provide some suggestions for cognitive group treatment.

Cognitive group can be a particularly appropriate group for the clinical neuropsychologist to design and deliver. A cognitive group can also be co-led with a speech pathologist or with another psychologist. The fees for this service can be billed under the new Health and Behavior evaluation and management codes, linked with your patients' medical diagnoses. (See Appendix H for codes.) If you have little experience in conducting group therapy of any kind, you can prepare by reading the literature, and by obtaining consultation from a neuropsychologist or psychologist who is experienced in such groups. This will be time and money well invested in your training. Your ability to understand and manage the process of group screening and treatment will facilitate your effectiveness in leading such groups—and it will increase your satisfaction and enjoyment.

WHICH PATIENTS?

In the group treatment example I describe in this chapter, you already know the clinical goal of your group: You want to teach patients with acquired brain injury or disease how to understand and manage their thinking and communication deficits more effectively.

The next step in the process of creating a group is determining which patient group(s) you want to include. Are you interested in including patients with a range of neurologic injury or disease, including those with TBI, tumor, stroke, anoxic brain damage? Or, do you want to include only one subgroup of patients with similar disorders? Do you want to include people who may have a progressive disease such as multiple sclerosis (MS)? What about patients with mild TBI or a persisting postconcussion syndrome? Keep in mind, as you consider these questions, that each of these patients will have different needs in the group. Don't burden yourself by taking on too much, too soon.

Some practitioners prefer groups in which the patients all have the same injury or illness. Other practitioners are more concerned that the patients share similar levels of abilities and deficits, regardless of injury or illness. Experienced practitioners can often manage a mix of diagnostic groups, but the pros and cons must be carefully weighed.

You may prefer to treat a particular age range of patients. You might create a group of younger patients and another group for middle-aged or older patients. Each group's life concerns are likely to be more homogeneous. For example the younger patient may not be as well established in his or her work and personal life, and may need extra time and attention to examine how one focuses on achieving success in life. The older patient may have already established a successful career or family life which has now been jeopardized: it is this well-established life that he or she is trying to re-establish.

Finally, some practitioners prefer groups of patients whose injuries or illnesses are more recent in onset, and who are still struggling to understand and begin to manage this new reality.

For some patients, being in a group with others who share their disease or injury is very important and they prefer not to be part of a diagnostically mixed group. I have been told for instance, by some patients with MS, that the sometimes relapsing/remitting, volatile, or progressive nature of their disease sets them apart. They feel that patients without MS cannot fully appreciate the challenges of unpredictable fluctuations in symptom severity, as well as the ultimately progressive, rather than improving, nature of their illness. You should consider these preferences when designing your groups.

While I am always open to these patient preferences, I think there is also much to be gained by patients when they encounter others whose diseases differ. Young patients with malignant brain tumors, for example, who are trying to live a life of quality and meaning in their limited remaining time, can be an important reality check for other members of the group, who may feel overwhelmed by their own changes in cognitive or physical function. Patients can develop an improved sense of perspective when they encounter someone whose plight is more severe than their own.

Multiple sclerosis patients suffer frustrating mixtures of fatigue, weakness, memory retrieval problems, and changes in executive functions but they may still notice how well they are able to express themselves in the group. They have the opportunity to observe, for example, a younger and healthier man with a severe brain stem injury, and its profoundly limiting effect on his motor and speech abilities.

Although it is a truism that there is always someone who has it better than you and someone else who has it worse, that is not the only lesson I hope group members will learn. I hope they learn an increased appreciation of the connection and commonality that humans share when we are engaged in any kind of serious struggle. This is not taught directly in a cognitive group. Rather, patients usually learn from the experience of being in the group. This experience is often a source of emotional strength that supports the willingness to take practical steps to more effectively cope with one's difficulties.

This awareness and acceptance of a common reality can also reduce feelings of isolation and aloneness that certainly afflict all humans. This bond with others is particularly important when a person's sense of self and full membership with humanity has been threatened by neurologic injury or disease. So, even when you don't set out to conduct group psychotherapy, any set of people in group treatment are likely to take away this kind of unspoken new learning.

There are also practical factors that play a role in patient selection and development of an effective cognitive group. For example, I do not have the luxury of time, space and staff to provide group treatments for patients by diagnoses. Thus, for many reasons, I have found that it is often effective to include a broad mixture of diagnostic groups, with varying levels of age and chronicity, as long as two conditions are met: The majority of the group members must have common problems and goals, and they must have common levels of basic abilities and deficits.

For example, you may lead a successful cognitive group with patients whose ultimate goal is either to return to some form of paid employment or to maximize their productivity in volunteer work settings. Although some patients have mild injuries and some more severe injuries, they are united by the common realities of being capable of working and able to learn and use compensatory techniques. Further, they share a common goal of achieving effective function in the workplace, which may also include improved social interactions.

BASIC CLINICAL RULES AND PROCEDURES

Patient Screening

Remember that this chapter is not intended as a substitute for a good grounding in group theory and practice if you do not have training or experience in group treatments. Consult with colleagues about their procedures. Some basic group member criteria I use for patients with brain injury or disease are as follows:

1. Basic new learning capacity is present.
2. Postinjury IQ levels are 75 or above (so patients can understand basic ideas).
3. Functional verbal comprehension and expression skills are present.
4. There is no active drug or alcohol abuse.
5. There is no history of assaultive or violent behavior, unless clear improvements have been maintained for 1 yr prior to entering the group.
6. No recent history of psychiatric hospitalization

Unless the patient is already well known to you or to a trusted colleague, it is important to hold a preliminary screening interview with them. Once you have satisfied yourself with respect to the above issues, you can proceed to have the patient sign a consent for treatment, supply you with necessary insurance information, and sign a form that indicates he or she will be responsible for fees.

Attendance, Participation, Confidentiality, Respect

I review the screening criteria with patients at the time of the screening interview, and again at the first meeting of the group. Thinking deficits are a very personal kind of loss, and the feedback from other patients is likely to be far more effective if people are familiar with norms of group behavior and have formed an attachment to each other and to the group leader. Patients are expected to attend each session, since their presence, participation, and observational skills are critical to the therapeutic value of the group. Each member depends upon the others. While there are the usual exceptions such as illness patients are obliged to let me know of any scheduling problems. Ideally, the patient will also mention this within the group, to let the other patients know in advance.

Although patients are expected to be present, involved, and as attentive as possible, they are not required to speak in the group, unless responding to questions. They are, of course, required to complete group assignments, and homework. Some patients—with varying degrees of aphasia, for example—may find it much easier and more comfortable to listen, and to speak only occasionally. Even so, they benefit from the group discussions and they can learn to incorporate new coping strategies into their daily lives.

Group confidentiality is essential. Patients must feel comfortable expressing themselves. I repeatedly remind members that confidentiality is expected from all participants: *Any* discussions that reveal information about any patients are not allowed to ever leave the group. There are no exceptions. While cognitive group members are welcome to take their notebooks and handouts home and to discuss the general themes and issues reviewed, they are not to reveal details of what other members have said nor the names of other group members.

I also caution people to be careful about initiating personal conversations with other group members in the waiting areas, where other patients or family members may be present. Those individuals do not feel bound by confidentiality, and should not be privy to information discussed in group.

Respect in the cognitive group setting is operationally defined as follows:

1. To listen when other members speak
2. To refrain from interrupting when others speak
3. To allow for differences of opinion
4. To refrain from hostile comments, including the use of sarcasm or name calling or accusations of personal failings
5. To refrain from whispering to one's neighbor when others are speaking
6. To turn off cell phones and pagers before entering the group
7. To avoid the use of sexually suggestive remarks or overly familiar social behaviors, such as inappropriately embracing or touching fellow patients
8. To refrain from hostile nonverbal behaviors, such as sighing, eye-rolling, or fidgeting when someone speaks

As you can see from the above, cognitive group can be quite lively and challenging, even when one has ostensibly gathered primarily to improve patients' attention, concentration, memory, reasoning, planning, and organizing skills. This is why basic group management skills are essential to effective group leaders. They can be learned with experience and a good co-leader.

Use of Co-Leaders

If you are a relatively inexperienced practitioner I encourage you to engage the services of a co-leader until you feel comfortable and effective. Furthermore, I think the use of co-leaders is always ideal, although it isn't always possible. Co-leaders add to the interest, range, and liveliness of your groups. They provide patients with two personalities with whom to interact and two sources of helpful feedback and cognitive rehabilitation ideas. A co-leader can help corral or restrain one or two difficult group members who may become disinhibited or otherwise socially troublesome. Having a co-leader makes this work far more manageable—and far less emotionally burdensome.

After a group meeting, it can be both interesting and supportive to brainstorm what did or didn't work, with your co-leader. Together, you can refine treatment plans, bring in other modifications or ideas, and discover what the other may have observed—that you missed—during a particular group session. A co-leader may bring knowledge in a particular specialty, and you have the opportunity to both learn more yourself and to receive support from your colleague. Finally, having a co-leader means that group members are being recruited from two practices, which may help to keep your cognitive group thriving. A co-leader may have a slightly different patient population, or have a slightly different set of referral sources, all of whom can be educated about the treatment options the two of you offer together. Finally, working alongside a co-leader can also help reduce the inevitable isolation of the individual private practice setting.

Individual Therapy as an Adjunct to Group Therapy

Sometimes when I have screened patients referred for cognitive group, I have identified some whose prior psychiatric history is significant, or whose current levels of depression or anxiety are problematic. At other times, it is clear that some long-standing characterologic vulnerabilities will make it difficult for a patient to withstand feedback in a group setting. The patient may have an acquired problem with suspiciousness or misperception. Or perhaps a patient has recently become painfully aware of the ways in which his or her cognitive abilities have changed, so discussion of cognitive deficits is likely to be particularly painful.

Yet any or all of these patients may need cognitive group treatment. And they will benefit if appropriate preparations can be made in advance. In a private practice setting, cognitive group patients may not be otherwise engaged in a full-time outpatient neurorehabilitation program, and you may need to compensate for this unmet need.

To adapt to this circumstance, I may require that, prior to being allowed to participate in cognitive group, patients establish adjunctive care, which will include psychotropic medications and psychotherapy. If I have concerns about patients' attendance or commitment, I may also require that they first establish a reliable record of participation in some other activity such as taking a class or seeing a psycotherapist. Naturally, such requirements depend upon the nature of the group.

If you are going to offer a class, advertised to the public, on the use of memory compensatory techniques as part of a Patient Education setting or model, these issues do not likely need to be addressed so rigorously. You collect your tuition in advance, people can attend or not attend as they wish, and it is a purely didactic approach.

If you intend to offer a treatment group brain-injured patients are expected to give each other feedback about thinking performances and to receive constructive criticism from you about how they affect others. Keep in mind the cognitive and affective burden this places on these patients when you develop—and enforce—your group treatment guidelines.

BASIC BILLING AND DOCUMENTATION

Our cognitive group meets for two hours each week for eight consecutive weeks. I bill cognitive group treatment under the Health and Behavior Codes for group treatment (see Appendix I). I bill 4 units, at 15 minutes per unit, for the 60 minutes of the group that I lead.

My co-leader is a speech and language pathologist, who bills for her time as part of a speech therapy group code. She bills for the 60-minutes portion that she leads.

My part of cognitive group involves teaching and discussion of ways to compensate for common cognitive problems. The speech pathologist focuses upon communication issues, as well as a 'practice lab' for using many specific strategies in real-life circumstances.

We usually have 8 patients in our group. The reimbursement at this group size is reasonable, and helps to cover the extra time we spend in treatment planning outside of group and the cost of materials.

ONE MODEL FOR COGNITIVE GROUP TREATMENT

I have included in Appendix J a sample of some of our handouts from the typical cognitive group that the speech pathologist, and I currently co-lead.[1]

We also actively solicit formal feedback from patients at the end of each cognitive group session, so they can comment on the various handouts, tasks, and topics, to see what proved most helpful (or not) to them. As a result, our handouts have continued to evolve on a regular basis over time. You will likely find the same.

In the sample packet of materials (Appendix J), you will see that we provide patients with the following:

1. A statement of the purpose and goals of group
2. An outline of the 8 weeks, with topics listed for each week
3. Summary sheet of brain regions and associated deficits
4. Two pictures of the brain
5. Most commonly cited cognitive deficits related to acquired brain damage
6. A variety of other handouts (e.g., on attention, memory, general rules of good communication, time management strategies, and one useful approach to planning and organizing project completion).

It is also important to note that cognitive groups work best with a set of in-group activities where, for example, patients can try out new skills together and can develop problem solutions together.

For example, in one group we often used a "telegram" task to help patients practice getting the main idea and improve the efficiency of their spoken communications. A lengthy paragraph is provided in spoken or written form. The patients are asked to winnow this down to 10–15 key words, yet still convey the essential features of the message. They brainstorm together in the group, experiment with different key words or ideas, and come to agreement on the best summary of the paragraph's message.

Depending upon your patients' cognitive problems, and upon what you consider to be important cognitive strategies, your group content may differ from some of these examples. This sample approach is intended only to stimulate your thinking.

[1]You are welcome to use these copyrighted materials as guides for your groups, but they cannot be sold for profit by you or by any organization, individual, or group of individuals.

EXERCISES

1. *Do I have the necessary training and expertise to offer a cognitive group to patients?*
2. *If not, from whom can I obtain the necessary training and supervision or co-leadership support?*
3. *What population of patients do I prefer to treat?*
4. *What format do I like best for groups (e.g., once a week for 90 minutes or 2 hours, or twice a week for 45–60 minutes)?*
5. *What is the minimum number of patients to make this clinically effective?*
6. *How many weeks would I like my group to meet?*
7. *Do I want this to be a patient education type of group or a cognitive therapy group?*
8. *How should I market this group and to whom?*

14

RESEARCH AS A DAILY REALITY

When you establish your own private practice, you have a unique opportunity to craft hypotheses about neuropsychological populations that interest you and to record information from your data summary sheets in order to automatically track pertinent variables. While respecting patient confidentiality and safeguarding patient privacy every step of the way, as a private practitioner you won't have to wait 6 months for approval from a human subjects review board to analyze data sitting in your file cabinets.

WHAT ARE YOUR RESEARCH INTERESTS?

In the initial phases of establishing a private practice, some practitioners want any and all referrals, regardless of diagnostic group. Although this is understandable, it is probably in your best interest to define at least some broad categories of your expertise and interest. Not only will you be able to provide the best possible evaluations for your patients and their referring providers, you will also be able to focus from the outset on research questions that interest you.

For example, I was curious about two very broad groups of patients: (a) adult patients ages 16–65 who had an acquired neurologic problem or injury, and who were interested in resuming productive work or school activity; and (b) any patient suspected of having a possible dementing condition. I tended not to see many patients with primary motor disorders, with Parkinson's disease, Huntington's disease, or older (>65) patients with stroke, unless multi-infarct dementia was suspected.

Instead, I evaluated many working age patients with head injury, tumor, aneurysm, arteriovenous malformation and anoxic injuries. I also evaluated adults with lifelong learning disability or attention deficit disorder that had never been thoroughly addressed, and I evaluated patients with dementia. As time passed, I also began to receive more referrals for evaluation of patients with suspected somatoform or conversion disorders, in the context of very mild or even questionable concussive injuries.

These populations were well suited to my three broad clinical and research interests: (a) long-term return-to-work outcome following adult-onset neurologic illness or injury; (b) patterns of performance and disease progression associated with the dementias, especially Alzheimer's disease; (c) the role of premorbid personality variables and strengths in determining outcome following injury or illness.

What Are Your Populations of Interest?

You may not yet know what research question is going to be of interest to you. For example, I have been aware of the cognitive problems many multiple sclerosis patients have, but I had never evaluated sufficient numbers of them to allow for population studies. However, I now have a large data set with over 200 patients with MS. The opportunity is now there to track return-to-work issues in this population, and, for example, to see what cognitive problems might be associated with poor work outcome, even in people who are not severely physically impaired.

Most neuropsychology practitioners have the opportunity over time to expand their services to new populations of patients. You may start out with patient diagnostic groups for whom you had the most training in graduate school, internship, or fellowship. You may have also had institution-based experience prior to deciding to establish a private practice and so you may have learned about additional neurodiagnostic groups in that setting.

There may also be patients in unfamiliar diagnostic groups available for you to see in the area where you are going to set up your private practice. You will need to learn all you can about these patients and their problems.

In general, the same basic research plans and methodologies should serve you well for any patient population, especially if you routinely collect reliable data on demographic, testing, medical, premorbid education and outcome variables. If you can guarantee patient confidentiality, you do not have to obtain prior permission to analyze and report those results.

How to Arrange Research Access to Patient Populations

During the marketing phase of your practice development, let potential referral sources know your areas of research interest. Tell them a bit about what is known about such patients and why you want to investigate further. Some of your colleagues may be interested in collaborating with you. Be open, as well, to considering research studies on patients that are of interest to potential referral sources.

If you are working part-time in an institutional setting while you establish your private practice, visit the various departments, physicians, nurses, and therapists who see the patients you are interested in evaluating or treating, and offer your neuropsychological services.

Marketing brochures can include information about your research interests. Read colleagues' marketing materials to learn of collaboration potential. For example, I recently received a brochure from a clinical psychologist who has an interest in adolescents and young adults with a diagnosis of Asperger's syndrome. In addition to the clinical work and group treatments he is providing for those patients, there is potential for collaborative research with these patients because, coincidentally, I am seeing more of those young adults in my practice. Child-based services are no longer appropriate for them, and they don't have well-established supports or treatment programs as older adolescents or young adults. Their patterns of impairment and ability on neuropsychological evaluation are quite compelling. This is a great clinical research opportunity: Can one achieve behavioral change and improved psychosocial outcomes in this population, depending upon the relative pattern of neuropsychological abilities and deficits, and the kind of group treatment they receive?

Setting up Your Hypotheses

Are you interested in descriptive studies that may contribute neuropsychological information on a little known population? Or, for example, would you prefer to study specific types of memory or language dysfunction within a particular population?

Perhaps you are interested in a controlled treatment study in which, for example, you investigate the possibility of improvements in neuropsychological function in patients with a particular disease. Or you might investigate the role of specific neuropsychological variables in predicting who will benefit from an intervention. Based on the literature and your clinical experience you may determine which are critical cognitive or behavioral factors in the disease or injury. For example, you may want to predict which areas of test performance or behavioral function you would expect to improve following treatment. This kind of study can be a collaboration with colleagues who are providing treatment to patients that you have evaluated.

Consider the test instruments or neurobehavioral problems you find curious or thought-provoking in your daily work with patients. What are possible ways to explore these observations and questions systematically? Proceeding on your natural interest makes it vastly more rewarding to review the literature discuss, your findings with colleagues, and plan studies as part of your clinical work.

Setting up Your Data Summary and Data Entry Sheets

When you design a data summary form, think of it as a data entry sheet with enough detail on variables of interest to allow for consistent and thorough data collection from each of your patients. There may be certain core test scores that you collect from almost all of your patients between the ages of 18 and 60, for example, Wechsler Adult Intelligence Scale-III subtest scores, Wechsler Memory Scale-Revised scores, Trails A and B, and verbal fluency scores. At the very least, you will have an interesting set of variables with which to associate the age, education, gender, medical diagnoses, level of impairments, and average IQ values for your patient population. This can be very useful from a practice patterns standpoint when you want to review the populations being referred to you, by whom, and which providers you may want to cultivate further. In this instance, your data serve as a source of program evaluation. They offer potential guidance for the further development of your private practice, even if you have no other desire to publish or conduct research.

Consider designing your data summary sheets so a graduate student could enter the information into a spreadsheet. There are also voice data entry systems that allow you to speak, rather than type, your variables into the computer, so you can very quickly and accurately enter large amounts of information in relatively little time.

You may discover that a particular test has not been well standardized for a particular age, ethnic, or educational group. If you have already been collecting data on all tests administered to all of your patients, it is relatively easy to retrieve those files and review the data. You may discover an interesting relationship, or you may develop hypotheses which you can subsequently test which, leads you to then further investigate these tests. For example, you may observe a significant disparity between test scores within a particular population of patients, compared to other subgroups. For example, problems on the Rey Osterrieth Complex figure may occur early in the course of dementia for certain Alzheimer's patients but not for others with this disease—why not?

Consistent collection of test from all of your patients can benefit a private practitioner: It may help future research investigations. The results may have a direct bearing upon your clinical practice. They may help the rest of us better understand a particularly puzzling cognitive or testing issue.

Finding a Graduate Student Assistant

Over my years of practice, I have been approached a number of times by graduate students who had heard me give lectures. These students were interested in learning more about patients with brain impairments. They also hoped to be able to gain access to neuropsychological data for a master's projects or doctoral dissertations. This ultimately led to a dissertation project that provided one student with data, and provided me with information about the average IQs and MMPI profiles of the mildly, moderately, and severely brain injured patients referred for neuropsychological evaluation prior to treatment. To find a graduate student, you can post announcements seeking students who are interested in research projects at colleges and universities.

Regardless of your setting, you need to follow ethical and legal guidelines for the protection of patient confidentiality. Once those requirements have been met it is a relatively easy matter to allow a student to collect and analyze demographic and neuropsychological information under your supervision. In return, the student can enter data that is also of interest to you for future projects or program evaluation purposes.

GRANTS

I don't have the time or interest to write grant proposals as a primary investigator. However, I do have the time and interest to assist colleagues as a co-investigator on a subject in grant funded research. For example, a colleague was interested in the effect that certain chemotherapy agents might have on the treatment of women with breast cancer, and most specifically in the effect those agents might have upon mood and cognition. As a co-investigator, on one project within the larger grant I will provide neuropsychological screening both pre- and posttreatment. My time in screening these patients will be paid as will the psychometrists' time, which support the feasibility of this kind of study while simultaneously carrying a heavy clinical load. I benefit further by being better informed. You may want to explore such opportunities.

You might offer to collaborate with colleagues whose research interests are known to you. Be prepared with literature reviews to persuade them, for example, that examining the neuropsychological features of certain populations can add considerably to the value of their studies. Alternatively, you might demonstrate ways to expand those studies to maximize future funding.

CONFERENCE PRESENTATION

Take advantage of invitations to present at international, national, state, and local conferences. Your state psychological association needs the participation of a wide range of speakers to keep topics fresh for its constituents. Neuropsychological topics are often of interest to the general practitioner. For example, defining typical cognitive, personality, and neurobehavioral changes that may accompany certain kinds of injuries (e.g., TBI) or illnesses (e.g., dementia) is likely to be useful for clinicians.

At any level, i.e., local, state, national or international, you may wish to report your study of a diagnostic group or testing tool. If you have a treatment specialty such as group treatment for patients with acquired brain injury, this is likely to be useful to other neuropsychology practitioners. If you are affiliated with a university that has postdoctoral training in neuropsychology or rehabilitation psychology, you may offer a seminar on establishing or cooperatively operating such training programs.

Public speaking about your work requires a level of knowledge and preparation that can provide you with the basis for a journal article or book chapter. More, the preparation for a presentation can lay the groundwork for both future speaking engagements and for the subsequent publication of your presentation.

JOURNAL ARTICLES

Before you submit a journal article, ask several colleagues to review it. This will maximize the chances that your subsequent submission will be given serious review and that it will pass that review. If you have mentors or colleagues who serve on journal editorial boards, ask them about the process, and ask if the journal reviewers at their publication have a particular interest. If you receive editorial feedback that you don't entirely understand, be sure to speak to the editors and to colleagues for clarification. If you are persistent and if you resubmit your carefully revised manuscript, you are likely to eventually be published.

CHAPTERS

Book chapters are requested by the book's editor. Your chances of being included in such invitations are improved considerably if you establish mastery of a specialty, participate in conferences, make presentations, and publish journal articles. The process is further helped if you become active in your national, state, or local professional organizations or otherwise become known to like-minded colleagues, some of whom may one day edit a book.

You don't need to remain, passive, however. If you have an interest in editing a book, you can approach publishers on your own and submit a book proposal. You might speak to colleagues who have edited books. Ask how they went about it.

JOURNAL GROUPS

I can't possibly keep up with all that is published, sometimes not even within a fairly narrow topic area. However, journal clubs are likely to be helpful for every neuropsychologist, because each month a colleague takes the responsibility for reading and summarizing articles of general interest. Journal clubs can be even more useful for private practitioners. For one, you may not be as routinely exposed to continuing education opportunities when you are not part of a university or medical school setting, where so many speakers, classes, and training opportunities are built into the fabric of your day and setting. The monthly review with peers of a particular article will usually ensure that you read the article. Even if you don't, you will still benefit by being exposed to a summary and discussion.

If you are in a solo private practice, isolation from peers can be a problem. Journal clubs provide a satisfying format for meeting with other private practitioners. If you have a university affiliation as well, it is a relatively easy matter to learn when your colleagues hold their monthly journal club meeting. Often, psychology residents or fellows are also present at these meetings, and their enthusiasm, energy, and challenging questions add to the quality of the discussion.

COLLABORATIONS

As you can see, even in a chapter about ways to keep research activities alive and well in your clinical practice, collaboration with like-minded colleagues can be an essential component of success. Sometimes, just having one or two professional allies with whom you can meet and discuss the latest studies will make a substantial difference for your future presentations and publications.

One final caveat about collaboration. Sometimes when clinicians gather, especially if they have not had much opportunity to get together otherwise, the journal article discussion or even journal article preparation can segue into a general case conference or gabfest. Although both of these may be needed and helpful, given the nature of your past week or month, they don't help with progress on the topic or project at hand. It is usually best to agree to commit the first 75% of the time you have together to focus on the purpose of the meeting, and then leave the remain 25% of the time for general riotous discussion.

You may discover that you need to set aside two meeting times per month, one for research and one for case discussions with peers. But even in the midst of case discussions, stay alert to the opportunities you have right in front of you as source material for teaching and publication. A series of well-selected, well-crafted cases can be a valuable future conference presentation or journal artical or publication.

EXERCISES

What populations or questions interest you?

Generate data summary sheets that would allow someone to enter data directly into a computer program.

If you were to speak to a group, what topic would you choose?

Research and then outline such a presentation, based upon your literature review and your clinical experience.

Submit this presentation at your next conference opportunity.

Who is a like-minded colleague in your area, or anywhere? Email bridges long distances, and good collaboration doesn't require physical proximity. Contact that person and see if she or he has an interest in collaborating.

Speak to one mentor or colleague who is on an editorial board to learn if he or she has advice for manuscript submission.

15

SUMMARY AND CONCLUSIONS

As you prepare to launch into independent private practice, let's review the key principles and ideas we have explored.

THE IMPORTANCE OF RELATIONSHIPS AND MUTUAL "BEST INTEREST"

As I look back over in this book, two guiding principles emerge: Do good work and develop positive relationships. The most successful private practices depend, not surprisingly, upon good interrelationships with referral sources, patients and their families, and with colleagues in other practices or settings. Although it isn't possible to agree with everyone at every moment, if you are competent, fair, and generous in your approach to others, you will find opportunities for work will return to you in multiplicative fashion.

Mutual best interest is a valuable goal in any setting, and private practice is no exception. Determine what outcomes, goals, procedures, and processes are in your best interest for every facet of your business. At the same time, remember that an important part of your best interest is insuring that others are being treated fairly, as well. This includes patients, referral sources, colleagues, employees, your family, and yourself.

WHAT SORT OF WORK DO YOU WANT TO DO?

Review the aspects of practice that you like the most and feel most competent providing. Is there a need for this emphasis in your area? Speak to possible referral sources, to neuropsychologists within institutions, and learn with what populations it might make most sense to begin. For example, should you open an evaluation practice specializing in adolescents who had serious injuries or neurologic problems as children, but who are now age 17–18? They will need assistance with transitions to independent living and employment. Or might you establish a working relationship with your state or local department of vocational rehabilitation and become a primary provider of evaluation or treatment?

It may take a number of years of experience to determine the populations and the types of practice activities you most enjoy. However, if you keep the question in mind, your chances of finding the right niche for your skills are greatly improved. Although there are always practical considerations, wouldn't you want to enjoy at least 51% of your work? Otherwise, why are you doing this? If you take on the challenges of self-employment, make sure that you will enjoy your work.

WHERE AND HOW DO YOU WANT TO BEGIN?

While you are gradually building your own practice base, do you want to establish a part-time practice within an institution or do you prefer contract work? Or, have you already been planning this transition, and are you ready now to proceed with your own full-time private practice? What are the sources of your referrals likely to be? Do you want to combine evaluation, treatment, and teaching activities?

Have you established a realistic time frame for practice development? How long did it take other practitioners in your area to get started? Did they have unique advantages that you may not have? What is a realistic estimate of hours per week your various activities are going to require?

Although it takes time to build clinical hours, your marketing, in-services training, teaching, and practice development activities are likely to be taking significant portions of your first weeks and months. You may spend a lot of time initially trying to generate business, before you generate income-producing referrals. Have you considered how you will maintain your confidence during this phase?

WHAT IS THE BEST WAY TO MINIMIZE COSTS AND MAXIMIZE INCOME?

Have you done everything you can to keep fixed costs low? Are you going to share space or barter services for the use of an office? Can you conduct testing for a colleague for use of her office and test materials 1 or 2 days a week in return?

Are you prepared for billing and collections? Insurance companies typically pay between 50–80% of the hourly fee they allow for neuropsychological services. They often allow $80–90 an hour for testing. Is this clearly explained in your patient consent to treatment forms, and will you collect a reasonable payment in advance for your services? You must, at a minimum, collect enough money in advance to cover your cost of doing business, even if you are willing to wait for the balance of reimbursement from the insurance company and/or the patient.

WHAT SORT OF FINANCIAL FLOOR DO YOU NEED?

How much money will you actually need to collect each month in order to cover your expenses for the business? What income do you need to bring home to provide basic living expenses? Are you prepared to subsidize your business from sources other than actual collections during the first 6–12 months of establishing your private practice? What if it takes 2 years to become established, rather than 6 months? Do you have a plan B?

If you have equity in a house, perhaps now is the time to establish a line of credit at a low interest rate. This may be facilitated if you are currently employed in an institutional setting, or have a regular full or part-time salary. You can then borrow from your credit line if needed, at low interest rates, and deduct the interest you pay throughout the years as part of your mortgage interest.

HOW WILL YOU MONITOR AND PROMOTE GROWTH OF YOUR PRACTICE?

Do you have tracking systems in place to determine your best or most likely referral sources? What do you plan to do to increase your business? What sort of marketing strategy is most comfortable and most cost effective to you? Do you have a good plan for following up with referral sources, to determine if your feedback and report were helpful to them? What might they want or need other than what you provided?

How will you remain informed about opportunities to teach, collaborate on research projects, or provide vacation or maternity leave coverage at local institutions? Who can you speak to about developing these options? Think through all of these issues, brainstorm with colleagues or friends, and record your thoughts and ideas. Follow-up on these theoretical lists. Are the people and plans you have developed actually dependable?

WHAT DO YOU DO IF PLAN A ISN'T WORKING AS YOU EXPECTED?

If you aren't getting sufficient neuropsychological evaluation referrals, is it because there is a plethora of evaluators in your area? Are there not enough practitioners who provide therapy? If so, it might be more reasonable to establish a practice with a strong cognitive rehabilitation emphasis, doing only the occasional evaluation?

Do you need to apply to insurance panels, but can't do so now as a private practitioner? Do you want to regroup and provide contract services to local institutions or organizations to facilitate that membership?

Review the long list of income-earning possibilities you developed at the outset, and reconsider your priorities. Target items that you will aggresively develop now, while still allowing time for your outpatient evaluation practice to build.

WHAT ARE YOUR SHORT-TERM, INTERMEDIATE, AND LONG-TERM GOALS?

Year One: What do you hope to accomplish with respect to numbers of patients, referral sources, neuropsychological evaluations or other paid treatments, and reimbursed professional activities? What are realistic amounts for fees billed and fees collected? What do you estimate your direct and indirect expenses to be?

Are there a certain number of presentations, workshops, or professional meetings that you plan to attend? How many posters or clinical papers or workshops do you plan to present? Can you select the conferences that meet in areas that are less expensive for you to fly or drive to for that first year? Can you combine family vacation with such meetings in a way that allows you to deduct a portion of your expenses as part of the conference? This strategy can also reduce the amount of time you will be away from your family.

What do your particular practice activities and outcome data reveal? Based upon what you learn about year one results, where should you be investing your time and efforts for the next year or two or three?

Once you have practiced for several years, analyze the amount of energy you are expending and the revenue you are generating. Revisit the advantages and disadvantages of self-employment, as I described in earlier chapters. Sometimes even after you have established a good practice pattern and developed a steady income stream, you may decide that you need another change. Or, you may be satisfied with your results.

You may want to provide more or less of a given service, or see more or less of a particular population. I know competent people who have left lucrative full-time practices for a variety of good reasons. In one instance, the combination of patients that had emerged over time was a bi-modal distribution of litigating postconcussion patients or elderly dementing patients whose competency was being questioned. This practitioner was spending far more time in legal proceedings than he had intended when he set up his practice. He decided to secure a part-time position at a local clinic to perform neuropsychological evaluations for a wider range of patients. It was understood that he was not available to testify in forensic cases. He still maintained his private practice part time, in which he accepted the occasional competency or severe brain injury case, but he limited forensic cases to one per month.

PRACTICAL WAYS TO VARY YOUR PRACTICE

It is probably clear to you at this point that flexibility is an essential feature of my private practice model. Even though you may develop and maintain a particular service in relatively unchanged form over the course of your professional life, there are always features of any practice that may benefit from fine-tuning.

You may decide to alter the populations that you see or the way you conduct your evaluations. You may decide to expand and hire colleagues or assistants, so that your business can see more patients and can generate more business while still keeping to a reasonable turn-around time for appointments and reports. You may also decide to develop an entirely different enterprise, such as a series of training workshops, perhaps for health care providers who want to learn more about neuropsychological problems and management techniques for a particular patient population. You may occasionally serve as an instructor at a college.

In retrospect, it is clearer to me now that some of my long-term opportunities to earn income and vary my practice often presented themselves initially as requests from professional, charitable, advocacy, or patient groups for my free time and advice. Ten years ago, a colleague worked at a private free-standing rehabilitation company, in its early days of development. They did not have funds with which to hire a neuropsychology consultant. Because I liked the company and what they were trying to accomplish, I agreed to be available to staff for discussion of difficult cases at no charge. When they needed a neuropsychological evaluation, they sent the patient to see me. I enjoyed the contact, the cases, and the staff, and I considered this work as my way to donate something of value to the brain injury community.

Over the ensuing 10 years, that initial generosity on my part has led to many referrals for testing this company's patients, as well as the opportunity to formalize my role through contract work for consultation.

PERIODIC OR LONG-TERM CONTRACT WORK

Another interesting way to vary your practice and maintain a good income stream is to investigate locum opportunities within your professional community. Do institutions, medical centers, and private clinics who hire neuropsychologists know you are available to provide periodic coverage for a practitioner on extended leave, sabbatical, or vacation? In private practice, you may find it relatively easy to rearrange your schedule and accommodate 2 days a week for such coverage. You typically charge an hourly fee, and someone else is responsible for the billing and collections. You can generate steady income per week, with 16 hours onsite, and 4 hours at home to complete dictation or record review. Yet you still have 2 or 3 days in which to develop your private practice.

CLINICAL FACULTY APPOINTMENTS

I have recommended applying for an appointment to the clinical faculty at a medical center or university. This not only allows opportunities for teaching and research, but expands the pool of people who are familiar with your work and increases your opportunities for collaboration with like-minded peers. Find out as much as you can about faculty and programs. In addition to visiting websites, you can attend grand rounds presentations, ask questions, and follow-up with e-mails to the speaker.

Alternatively, you may wish to send a cover letter and curriculum vitae to psychology departments in universities or colleges, expressing interest in part-time teaching possibilities. Arrange for a follow-up interview with the department chair or a designated faculty person. By meeting in person you can learn more about what may be needed, now or in the foreseeable future, and you can let them know how you might be able to assist them. Teaching in any of a variety of settings is a source of stimulation and challenge and may contribute to the richness of your practice activities, access to students, and continuing education opportunities of your own.

BE ALERT TO CLINICAL, TEACHING, AND RESEARCH OPPORTUNITIES

Even if you have not had a long-standing interest in a particular research area, if you stay open to possibilities or invitations from colleagues, you will always have interesting new doors opening in your professional life. I have never, for example, worked closely with breast cancer patients. The cancer patients I evaluate typically have brain tumors. But, as you recall from chapter 14, I was approached by a colleague interested in both depression and cognitive problems in women undergoing chemotherapy for breast cancer. I didn't initially set out to study the systemic effects of cancer treatments but may have a grant-funded opportunity to do so. You may also not have set out to pursue a particular study or population or teaching opportunity. But when you hear the knock, consider opening the door. When given the chance to try something new, as long as it won't hurt you, saying "yes" will keep your life interesting and intellectually alive.

ENJOYING YOUR PRIVATE PRACTICE

Imagine what it might be like to have some creative ideas about establishing an evaluation practice or treatment programs, to have done the necessary planning and financial analysis, to see an opportunity, and to be free to act upon it. For some people, this is one of life's most exhilarating and rewarding moments: to have combined inspiration and successful application. You take the risk but you have control over the plans. You have the responsibility, but you also have a commensurate degree of authority to implement ideas, and to brainstorm a problem, rather than waste precious time in organizational futility. Imagine taking practical steps every day to grow your practice, without having to put your plan to a vote. You set your fees and no one raises or lowers them without your approval and consent. You don't have to see patients whom you consider unlikely candidates for positive results from either testing or treatment. You can be a truly independent practitioner.

The rewards are worth the effort. No matter what you ultimately choose, whether in long-term private practice, long-term institution-based work, or some combination of these or other activities, running your own business is a satisfying and invaluable lession in how things work. It is also an opportunity to learn what makes you happiest. If you ever return to the employ of others, you will be a better informed negotiator and you can better cope with the office politics that inevitably occur. Once you have been your own boss, once you discover that you can create and develop business for yourself, you are in a position of strength in any environment. More, you will appreciate the administration's problems, because you have been an administrator for an entire company—your own. And you also know how it feels to have everything clinical ultimately depending upon your skill and productivity because that is what paid the bills in your private practice life.

The flexibility in schedule that comes with private practice may single-handedly return more time to you than almost any other factor. Taking advantage of opportunities midweek to run errands or schedule personal appointments at times when traffic is light and most other people are at their jobs will restore at least a couple of extra hours of your week. A luxurious feeling comes with this ease and efficiency. (Remember when it only took 15 minutes to get from point A to point B? Well, on Wednesdays at 10 A.M., it still only takes that long.)

Reducing stress is an investment in your health. Initially, you may have more money worries when you are self-employed. However, once you have implemented your plan, you can begin psychologically to relax into the spaciousness of time. On fair weather days, you can visit the park, walk your dog, sit down and write a really good letter to your mother, have a leisurely lunch at home, fire up the espresso machine like Kinky Friedman does in his New York loft, pet the cat, and let the sun stream across your desk, while you take a moment to just breathe. You can even hop on the Nordic Trak for 20 minutes, without having to shower and dress again for the rest of the day, or pack and repack your gym bag, forgetting (always) some needed item for the office and the day.

When you venture out into the world in those free spaces of time that occur between 8 A.M. and 5 P.M., you will discover an entire other world of people who are no longer on the treadmill. You may find you now have time to spend with friends or family, time that is not painfully extracted when you are already totally exhausted. I have two good friends, both captured within institutional time at the moment, whom I have arranged to meet and whisk away one Friday a month for lunch at a local museum. They dash down the hospital steps to my waiting getaway car, and we are off for 75 minutes of pure fun. They get door-to-door service, I have the pleasure of driving, and we each get to connect, to eat, to laugh, to stay involved in each others' lives at a time when our parents are aging or dying, our children are growing up and away and we aren't too thrilled at the effect that gravity is having upon us. We share a dessert, wander through the galleries of new and old art, and revel in the universal aspects of life as revealed in these particular moments. We all return to our respective afternoons renewed and restored.

You may wonder why anyone would ever want to be anything other than self-employed. If those thoughts are running through your head, it is time to put them in motion. As I wrote at the outset of this book, I hope these ideas and experiences will prove a useful guide to you. To paraphrase P.J. O'Rourke: When people have freedom, and the rule of law, they will grow and thrive. Perhaps in a few years, you will be writing your own text on the subject of growing and thriving in self-employment. More power to you. And finally, as my grandmother would say if she was here with me to bid you well in your plans, "*Ciao . . . e buona fortuna.*"

APPENDIX A

NEUROPSYCHOLOGICAL EVALUATION REPORT FORMAT

IDENTIFYING INFORMATION

Name:
Age:
Date of birth:
Education:
Occupation:
Marital status:
Handedness:
Date of injury:
Date of exam:
Evaluated by:
Referred by:
Date of report:

REASON FOR REFERRAL AND PERTINENT MEDICAL BACKGROUND:

EXAMINATION PROCEDURES: What records were reviewed, who did interview and testing, who was present.

BEHAVIORAL OBSERVATIONS: Mental Status Exam (see Appendix L), patient appearance, effort, any special difficulties or thematic issues, comments on validity of testing.

INTERVIEW AND RELEVANT PERSONAL AND SOCIAL HISTORY: Who participated in the interview, did the person understand why they were being seen, what are the problems they spontaneously noted (see Appendix M).

SPECIFIC TESTS ADMINISTERED: List in column fashion

SUMMARY OF EXAMINATION FINDINGS:
(After two summary paragraphs of results, specific test scores and commentary are listed.)

DIAGNOSTIC IMPRESSION:

RECOMMENDATIONS:

Your Name
Title

cc list

APPENDIX B

WHAT IS A NEUROPSYCHOLOGICAL EVALUATION HANDOUT FOR REFFERAL?

NEUROPSYCHOLOGICAL EVALUATION
Description, Tests and Procedures, Costs, and Referral Guidelines

WHAT IS A NEUROPSYCHOLOGICAL EVALUATION?

A neuropsychological evaluation is an assessment procedure involving an in-depth interview, one-on-one testing, followed by test interpretation and report preparation, conducted by a licensed psychologist with a specialty in neuropsychology. It is also helpful if the neuropsychologist has had experience in rehabilitation of people with brain injuries.

The purpose of the exam is to identify the patient or client's brain-related areas of ability and deficit, and it is most commonly conducted following any kind of neurologically based change in function. This may be as a direct result of a traumatic brain injury, a stroke, a tumor, a degenerative condition such as multiple sclerosis, or some other disease or illness.

Neuropsychological evaluations are also helpful in identifying learning disabilities or attention deficit disorder in people who are otherwise healthy. Neuropsychological evaluations are also quite useful in discriminating psychiatric from neurologic problems, as underlying reasons for problems with memory, attention, or some aspects of problem solving.

WHAT COMPRISES THE FORMAL NEUROPSYCHOLOGICAL EVALUATION?

When a person is referred for evaluation, the neuropsychologist will do the following:

1. Review pertinent medical records and academic and work records where available.
2. Clarify referral questions as needed, so the neuropsychologist knows exactly what kind of information and recommendations would be helpful for the patient or client and the person requesting the evaluation.
3. Conduct an interview with the patient and one or more members of his or her family, and sometimes with teachers or employers
4. Administer and score a set of standardized tests, designed to assess many areas of thinking, behavior, and personality.
5. Prepare a thorough report, documenting the individual person's diagnosis strengths, weaknesses, and primary issues or challenges to adjustment and function, along with some detailed recommendations for how to improve function and adjustment.

NOTE: A psychometrist, or testing technician, is often used as an assistant in a neuropsychological evaluation. Psychometrists are trained to administer and score the standardized tests used in neuropsychological evaluations. They typically have bachelor's degrees or sometimes master's degrees and extensive testing experience.

The neuropsychologist gives a list of tests to be completed to the psychometrist, who then carries out or completes the testing battery. The neuropsychologist will instruct the psychometrist regarding which tests to use for a particular patient or client and when to use an easier or more difficult test for that particular person. The psychometrist also speaks directly to the neuropsychologist if testing questions or concerns arise during the test administration or scoring.

Psychometrists do not interpret the tests, nor do they decide which tests should be given. They are typically not present for the interview, nor for discussion of results. After completing the test administration, the psychometrist writes a set of behavioral observations to let the psychologist know important details about the client's behavior and reactions during testing.

WHAT TESTS ARE COMMONLY USED AS PART OF A TESTING BATTERY?

Most experienced neuropsychologists have a core battery of standardized tests that they administer to most patients, along with some selected tests, depending upon the specific needs of the client. It is fairly standard practice throughout the Pacific Northwest to administer the following core tests to adults and adolescents 16 years or older:

Wechsler Memory Scales (WMS-III) or WMS-R
Wechsler Adult Intelligence Scale—III (WAIS-III) or WAIS-R
Minnesota Multiphasic Personality Inventory (MMPI) or MMPI-2

All or part of the Halstead Reitan Neuropsychological Assessment Battery including any or all of the following:

Aphasia Screening Test (AST)
Trail Making Tests Parts A & B (Trails)
Category Test
Tactual Performance Test (TPT)
Finger Tapping Test (Tapping)
Sensory-Perceptual Exam
Grip Strength, Lateral Dominance Exam
Seashore Rhythm
Speech Sounds

Language and basic academic capacities are usually explored with the following tests:

Boston Naming Test
Controlled Oral Word Association Test (COWAT)
Animal Fluency Test
Wide Range Achievement Test—Form 3 (WRAT)
portions of the Boston Diagnostic Aphasia Examination (BDAE)
Gates MacGinitie Reading Comprehension Test or other reading Comprehension test
Estimates of pre-morbid IQ via single word reading tests (e.g., Wechsler Test of Adult Reading)

Attentional skills are assessed in a variety of ways, including using some of the subtests from the WAIS-R or WAIS-III scales and the WMS-R or WMS-III subtests. These could include the following:

Digit Span
Arithmetic
Mental Control

The following are also used:

Stroop Color Word Test
Paced Auditory Serial Addition Test (PASAT)

Memory testing, in addition to the WMS-R or WMS III and memory subtests within the Halstead-Reitan (e.g., Memory and Location from TPT) might include the following:

Fuld Object Memory Evaluation (FULD)
Selective Reminding Test (SRT)
California Verbal Learning Test (CVLT)
Benton Visual Retention Test (BVRT)
Rey Osterrieth Complex Figure delayed recall

There are also tests of malingering/effort given, including but not limited to the following:

The Hiscock
The Portland Digit Recognition Test
The Rey 15-Item Test with Delayed Recognition Test

These are not exhaustive lists of all possible tests, but include many of the standard and/or common tests used.

WHAT ARE GENERAL REFERRAL GUIDELINES?

1. If *return-to-work questions* are part of the overall need for assessment and treatment, neuropsychologists with experience in the area of rehabilitation may be particularly helpful.

2. If *differential diagnosis questions* such as possible psychiatric versus organic factors are critical, then a neuropsychologist whose background includes personality assessment along with clinical and psychotherapeutic experience may be very helpful.

3. In almost all instances of *acquired* brain injury, whether direct or indirect, via head trauma, tumor, stroke, electrocution, following severe myocardial infarction with loss of oxygen to the brain, AIDS-related dementia, postconcussion syndrome, suspected Alzheimer's disease, alcohol-related decline in capacity, or competency questions, *a baseline exam* should be obtained.

4. The *length and complexity of the evaluation will vary*, depending upon the patient's needs and issues, but some data are helpful in almost all cases. This baseline then allows for serial monitoring of recovery, improvement, or in some instances, decline, as well as providing specific information on strengths and weaknesses, useful in devising treatment, or in addressing other intervention questions.

5. On occasion, people may be *so severely impaired or incapacitated* as to render formal neuropsychological examination inappropriate, but discussion with a psychologist in advance of formal referral can often help clarify these issues, as well as *cross-cultural questions*.

6. From a *timing-of-exam* standpoint, with *severe head injury*, once the individual is emerging from the period of posttraumatic amnesia, a full formal exam can be considered. (Components of the exam may well be

used and administered during the course of hospital recovery, depending upon the patient, prior to resolution of posttraumatic amnesia.) For *less severe traumatic injuries (mild to moderate range)*, evaluation may be conducted within the first weeks or months after injury.

7. It is important to note that *reevaluations*, using the same psychometric instruments, repeated sooner than a minimum of 6 months apart, may be contaminated by practice effects.

ADDITIONAL USEFUL INFORMATION

1. The *length of time needed* to review records, interview the patient and his or her family, conduct the evaluation, score results, prepare a final report, and go over findings with the patient/client and/or referral source can vary quite a bit. Some psychologists do all of their own test administration, some employ psychometrists for this purpose, and some do a combination of their own testing augmented by psychometrist help.

2. The *final cost of an assessment* may also vary significantly, due to all of the factors noted above. In general, approximately $116–160/hour for this kind of evaluation can be expected in the Seattle area. Some companies and private practitioners charge a flat rate for a full neuropsychological evaluation, and these flat rate charges range from $1,700 to $3,000.

3. a. For most evaluations of outpatients with return-to-work issues or questions or psychiatric differential diagnosis concerns, one should expect an *average of 12–14 hours* overall evaluation time, depending upon the complexity of the case, the amount of pre-existing records, the speed with which the patient or client can complete testing, and so on.

b. In *forensic circumstances (legal cases)*, costs may increase, depending upon the amount of record review, need for consultation with attorneys, or interviews with collateral witnesses, teachers, employers, family members, or other neuropsychologists.

c. *Elderly or demented patients* usually require less time, in the range of 8 hours for testing and report preparation. Exceptions to this are likely to involve competency cases, where documents must be prepared for a court.

4. When *final determinations* about the amount of permanent, residual brain injury are needed, in cases of traumatic brain injury, one should allow *at least a period of 1 year, preferably 2, from the time of injury to the final* neuropsychological assessment before making final statements about the person's abilities and deficits.

5. *Establishing a working relationship with a neuropsychologist* you know and trust, who would be willing to help answer some of these questions as they arise, is in everyone's best interest, (i.e., the patient's and family's, the referral person's, the case manager's, and the neuropsychologist's).

For further information about neuropsychological or psychological evaluations, please feel free to contact Dr. Mary Pepping. I am happy to discuss general questions or specific cases with you on a preliminary basis at no charge.

Your Name ____________________

Business Address ____________________

Telephone No. ____________________

Fax No. ____________________

email address, if desired ____________________

APPENDIX C

DISCLOSURE STATEMENT AND INFORMED CONSENT

PROFESSIONAL QUALIFICATIONS

I received my doctorate in clinical psychology in 1981 from Washington State University. I completed a postdoctoral fellowship in neuropsychology at the University of Washington in 1982. I am licensed as a psychologist in the State of Washington (Lic. # PY 1252).

My practice currently includes neuropsychological and psychological evaluations of adults and adolescents. My testing approach incorporates elements of both quantitative and qualitative analyses of performance to determine what a person's abilities and difficulties might be, both in thinking and personality, and to assist with diagnostic questions and treatment recommendations.

WHAT IS A NEUROPSYCHOLOGICAL EVALUATION?

A neuropsychological evaluation is an assessment procedure, involving interview and testing, conducted by a licensed psychologist with a specialty in neuropsychology. It is also helpful if the neuropsychologist has had experience in rehabilitation of people with brain injuries.

The purpose of the exam is to identify the patient or client's brain-related areas of ability and deficit, and is most commonly conducted following any kind of neurologically based change in function. This may be as a direct result of a traumatic brain injury, a stroke, a tumor, a degenerative condition such as multiple sclerosis, or some other disease or illness.

Neuropsychological evaluations are also helpful in identifying learning disabilities or attention deficit disorder in people who are otherwise healthy. Neuropsychological evaluations are often quite useful in discriminating psychiatric from neurologic problems as underlying reasons for problems with memory, attention, or some aspects of problem solving.

When a person is referred for neuropsychological evaluation, the neuropsychologist typically does the following:

1. Reviews pertinent medical records, plus school and work records if the latter are available
2. Clarifies referral questions as needed, so the neuropsychologist knows exactly what kind of information and recommendations would be most helpful to all concerned.
3. Conducts an interview with the patient and one or more members of his or her family
4. Administers and scores a set of standardized tests, designed to assess important areas of thinking, behavior, and personality
5. Prepares a thorough report, documenting the individual person's strengths, weaknesses, and primary issues or challenges to adjustment and function, along with some detailed recommendations for how to improve function and adjustment
6. Sends copies of the report to the patient, to his or her physician, and to any other people that the patient requests receive a copy
7. Reviews results of report with person tested, their family, and others, as appropriate

Psychometrists (technicians who are trained to administer and score the standardized tests used, and typically have bachelor's or master's degrees, along with extensive testing experience) may also assist at times with testing. ______________ and ______________ are the psychometrists who assist Dr. Pepping.

POLICY

Appointments

If you are unable to keep an appointment, please call to cancel as soon as possible. A neuropsychological evaluation typically takes a full 8 hours for test administration, so a full day's time is saved for you. You will be charged a fee of $400 for appointments that are not canceled at least 24 hours in advance, except in the case of an emergency. Your insurance policy may not reimburse you for this charge.

Fees

Neuropsychological assessment is $150 per hour. A typical evaluation for people younger than age 65 takes 12–14 hours total time; for older adults, evaluations take approximately 7–8 hours total time. This time includes review of your medical records, the interview, administration and scoring of tests, discussion with your primary care physician as needed, interviews with family, teachers or employers, as appropriate, and preparation of a report summarizing the findings.

Insurance

Insurance companies vary considerably with respect to level of reimbursement for neuropsychological or psychological evaluations. In general, you should be prepared for the possibility that they will reimburse you no more than 50% of the fee they allow for a neuropsychological or psychological evaluation. We strongly recommend that you obtain specific confirmation in advance from your company regarding their coverage.

Northwest Psychology Associates cannot be responsible for trying to collect insurance reimbursement from your company. We will be happy to provide you with an insurance-appropriate copy of your bill that you can submit directly to your company for reimbursement. We require a 50% deposit from you at the time your examination is scheduled, and final payment when your report is ready.

My Availability

I am available from Monday through Thursday, at (---) ----- When you call, please leave some times when I might reach you. You may also try my cell phone at (---) -----.

In an emergency, you should call the Crisis Line or 911.

Your Record

State law requires that I maintain a written record of your evaluation and/or treatment. If at some time you desire that your record be reviewed by another licensed psychologist, it is your right to request in writing that I make the record available to that psychologist. You will be responsible for payment of a nominal fee for copying and transmitting the record. It is also your right to request corrections to the record.

Confidentiality

State law and ethical practice require that I must keep confidential your personal disclosures to me, except under the following circumstances:

If you specifically waive your right to confidentiality
If I believe you pose a harm to yourself or others
If I believe that a child or an elder is being abused, neglected, or molested

If your record is subpoenaed by a court
In order to facilitate your care by other clinicians

Your Rights as a Psychology Patient

You have the right to privacy of your psychological services.
You have the right to choose your psychologist.
You have the right to ask questions about your psychologist's services.
You have the right to discuss your services with anyone.
You have the right to terminate these services at any time.

If you believe your rights have been violated or that you have otherwise been mistreated by a psychologist, you may file a formal complaint with the Washington State Examining Board of Psychology:

Examining Board of Psychology
P. O. Box 47868
Olympia, WA 98504-7868
360 753-3095

YOUR AGREEMENT

I have read and agree to the above policy. I hereby give my informed consent for treatment, and to payment of bills I incur.

____
Your First Name Middle Name Last Name

____
Your Signature Date

____
Mary Pepping, Ph.D.

APPENDIX D

NORTHWEST PSYCHOLOGY ASSOCIATES

Mary Pepping, Ph.D. • Joseph Barber, Ph.D.

INTAKE REGISTRATION INFORMATION

Today's Date____________________

Name___________________________Date of Birth______________

Address________________________________Soc. Security#________

____

City State Zip Code

Home Phone_____________May I call you at this number?__________

Work Phone_____________May I call you at this number?__________

REFERRING PERSON:____

Address ____

Office Phone____

INSURANCE INFORMATION

Name of Insured___________________________Date of Birth________

Patient's relationship to insured person__________________________

Primary Insurance Company___________________________________

Address ____

Telephone Number____

Subscriber ID_________________________Group Number___________

Subscriber's Social Security #_________________________________

Patient's Driver's License Number______________________________

APPENDIX E

NORTHWEST PSYCHOLOGY ASSOCIATES

Mary Pepping, Ph.D. • Joseph Barber, Ph.D.

RELEASE OF INFORMATION

I,____________________________, give permission to Mary Pepping, Ph.D., to obtain the results of any evaluations and/or treatments from my therapists, rehab specialists, attendants, physicians, and/or attorneys concerning my condition, and to discuss my test results, needs, treatment recommendations, and progress with them.

____

Name (Printed)

____

Signature

____

Date

____

Witnessed by:

APPENDIX F

NEUROPSYCHOLOGY FEES FOR SERVICE

Record Review
Interview with Patient and/or Family
Evaluation Time (Testing and Scoring)
Report Preparation

All of the above services are billed at $150 per hour.

The typical neuropsychological evaluation, including all of the above, takes approximately 12–14 hours, and costs $1800–2100.

The typical psychological evaluation takes 9–11 hours total time, and costs approximately $1350–1650.

LEGAL CONSULTATION

Deposition time
Court appearances
Consultation with attorney

The above three services are billed at $400 per hour.
Deposition time is billed at a minimum of 2 hours ($800).
Court appearances are billed at a minimum of 4 hours ($1,600).

Payment in advance is required for Legal Consultation.
Checks should be made out to [your company name]
Federal Tax ID_____________

CANCELLATION POLICY

At least 3 full business days notice is required for cancellation of appointments. A $400 fee is otherwise required for last-minute cancellation of neuropsychological or psychological evaluations. Full fee payment is required for last-minute cancellation of legal appointments.

APPENDIX G

BILLING FORM
YOUR COMPANY NAME HERE
ADDRESS, PHONE AND FAX

Date

Statement of Professional Services

Patient:

Date of Birth:

Referring Physician:

Name of Insured:

Relationship to Patient:

Group No.:

ID or SS#:

Billing Period:

Diagnosis: ____

____

Date of Service	Procedure	Duration	Charge

Total: $

Provider

Charges are due and payable upon Receipt.
Please make checks payable to [name of your company].
Federal Tax ID:

APPENDIX H

COMMON INTERNATIONAL STATISTICAL CLASSIFICATION OF DISEASES—9TH REVISION CODES

Age-related cognitive decline 780.90
Alcohol abuse 305.00
Alzheimer's disease 331.00
Aneurysm, nonruptured 437.30
Anoxic brain damage 348.1
Brain abscess 324.0
Brain tumor, malignant 191.0
Brain tumor, unspecified 239.6
Carbon monoxide poisoning, toxic effects 986.00
Cerebellar degeneration, primary 334.20
Cerebral vascular disorder, unspecified 437.90
Cerebral vascular disorder, late effects 438.00
Concussion, no loss of consciousness (LOC) 850.0
Concussion, LOC $<$ 1 hr 850.1
(also see listings for Traumatic brain injury)
Delirium due to general medical conditions 293.00
Dementia due to general medical conditions 294.10
Disorder of Central Nervous System, not otherwise specified (NOS) 349.90
Encephalitits, Viral, Late Effects 139.00
Encephalopathy 348.30; Toxic encephalopathy 349.81
Epilepsy, unspecified 345.90
HIV/AIDS 042.00
Huntington's disease 333.40
Meningitis 322.90
Mental retardation 319.00
Multiple sclerosis 340.00
Neurocognitive disorder, mild 780.90
Parkinson's disease 332.00
Pick's dementia 331.10
Traumatic brain injury, no LOC 854.01

Traumatic brain injury, < 1 hour LOC 854.02
Traumatic brain injury, 1–24 hr LOC 854.03
Traumatic brain injury, > 24 hr LOC 854.04
Transient ischemic attack 435.90

To order your own ICD-9, Call Medicode, at 801-536-1000; FAX 800-536-1011

APPENDIX I

CURRENT PROCEDURAL TERMINOLOGY CODES

Codes listed are those I recommend using for patients with primary medical diagnoses. For a full listing of all possible codes, obtain a copy of the American Medical Association (AMA) Current Procedural Terminology (CPT) book, most recent edition.

To order, call the AMA at 1-800-621-8335.

Unless you have a prearranged contract or agreement, such as with your state's worker compensation carrier, that indicates codes 90801 (Diagnostic Interview) and/or code 96100 (MMPI-2 administration and scoring) will be covered for your brain-injured patients, those codes will otherwise be considered (by private insurance companies) as part of your patient's mental health plan. They then must be linked to a primary psychiatric diagnostic code, or the billing will not be accepted. I urge you to use the appropriate medical codes for your brain-injured patients, and to bill neuropsychological evaluation as 96117.

96115 Neurobehavioral screening exam. Clinical assessment of thinking, reasoning, judgment, acquired knowledge, attention, memory, visual spatial skills, language functions, planning, with interpretation and report, per hour.

96117 Neuropsychological Testing Battery. (e.g., Halstead-Reitan, Luria, WAIS-III) with interpretation and report, per hour.

NEW Health and Behavioral Assessment/Intervention Codes. Health and Behavioral Assessment and Intervention codes are used to identify or modify the psychological, behavioral, emotional, **cognitive** [my emphasis], and social factors important to the prevention, treatment, or management of **physical health problems** [my emphasis]. The focus of the assessment (or treatment) is not on mental health, but on the biopsychosocial factors important to physical health problems, their assessment, and/or treatment.

I encourage you to obtain a copy of the CPT code book to better appreciate the nuances of billing, but the following are the allowable codes.

HEALTH AND BEHAVIORAL ASSESSMENT/ INTERVENTION CODES

Please note: These codes must be billed in units that represent 15-minute increments. So, 1 hour of time spent is billed as 4 units.

Codes 96150–96155 describe services associated with an acute or chronic illness (not meeting criteria for a psychiatric diagnosis), prevention of a physical illness or disability, and maintenance of health, not meeting criteria for a psychiatric diagnosis, or representing a preventive medicine service.

Do not report codes 96150–96155 in addition to codes 90801–90899 on the same date.

96150 Health and behavior assessment. This can include a health-focused clinical interview, behavioral observations, psychophysiological monitoring, or health-oriented questionnaires, each 15 minutes of face-to-face contact with the patient, and part of an initial assessment

96151 Reassessment

96152 Health and behavior intervention—individual

96153 Group treatment (2 or more patients)

96154 Family (with patient present)

96155 Family (without patient present)

97532 Cognitive Rehabilitation—individual—15-minute increments It is reportedly still allowed by some insurance companies, but not all—it would be worthwhile to have the patient check with their insurance companies before using it.

APPENDIX J

SAMPLE COGNITIVE GROUP HANDOUTS

COGNITIVE GROUP

Purpose

To improve thinking, speaking, and comprehension skills in everyday interactions.

Goals

1. Develop and use consistent memory compensatory techniques.
2. Improve planning, organizing, and time-management skills.
3. Write more effective and accurate notes.
4. Fine-tune interpersonal communication style.
5. Clarify understanding of cognitive strengths and weaknesses.
6. Improve comprehension and recall of discussions in group interaction.
7. Explore additional topics of interest.

COGNITIVE GROUP OUTLINE

Week One

Introduction of members and purpose of group
Anatomy review and education
Attention—What is it, how does it work? (handout)
Daily schedules
Review Daytimer systems—discuss pros and cons of types
Homework assignments

Week Two

Review of Week One—anatomy, Daytimers, attention
Fine-tuning memory strategies and use of Daytimer
Memory—types and problem examples (handout)
Prospective memory discussion and assignments
Discuss use of different memory systems
Memory activities
Homework assignments

Week Three

Review of Week Two—Memory
Effective note taking
Story telling and transmission (videotaped)
Homework assignments

Week Four

Review note taking and videotape
Identify positive and negative methods of communication
Tangentiality—straying from the topic
Hyperverbality—increased talkativeness
Speed of thinking or information processing
Asking questions to slow down a speaker
Homework assignments

Week Five

Review of communication guidelines and issues
Begin discussion of planning and organizing
Routines, schedules, and time management
Write out a weekly schedule
Homework assignment—What is your toughest area to keep organized?
Develop a written plan to address it.

Week Six

Review of planning, organizing, time management
Individual cognitive strengths and weaknesses lists
Prospective memory assignments—more practice
Homework: Prepare a 5-minute speech for next week

Week Seven

Review of cognitive strength and weakness lists
An in-depth look at interpersonal communication skills (e.g., topic maintenance, turn taking, being aware of your listener)
Homework assignments

Week Eight

Requested topics of cognitive and communication interest

SUMMARY OF BRAIN AREAS AND DEFICITS FOLLOWING DAMAGE

Mary Pepping, Ph.D.

Frontal Lobe Damage (varies by Left Versus Right Hemisphere)

Reduced attention and concentration
Problems with planning and organization
Tangentiality
Hyperverbality
Easily distracted in normal environments
Trouble getting the main idea or point of a discussion
Subtle word-finding difficulties

May be a bit childlike or immature in behavior
Socially inappropriate at times
Impulsivity
Problems with judgment
Poorly controlled laughing or crying
Lack of sensitivity to other people's feelings
Lack of awareness of deficits or of impact on others

Temporal Lobe Damage (Varies by Left Versus Right Hemisphere)

Memory problems for new information—verbal versus spatial information
Reduced comprehension of the read or spoken word
Changes in melodic or musical capacity
Misperception of events
Possible visual disturbances
Heightened irritability
Rage reactions—limbic dyscontrol
Suspiciousness (especially when linked with parietal injury)

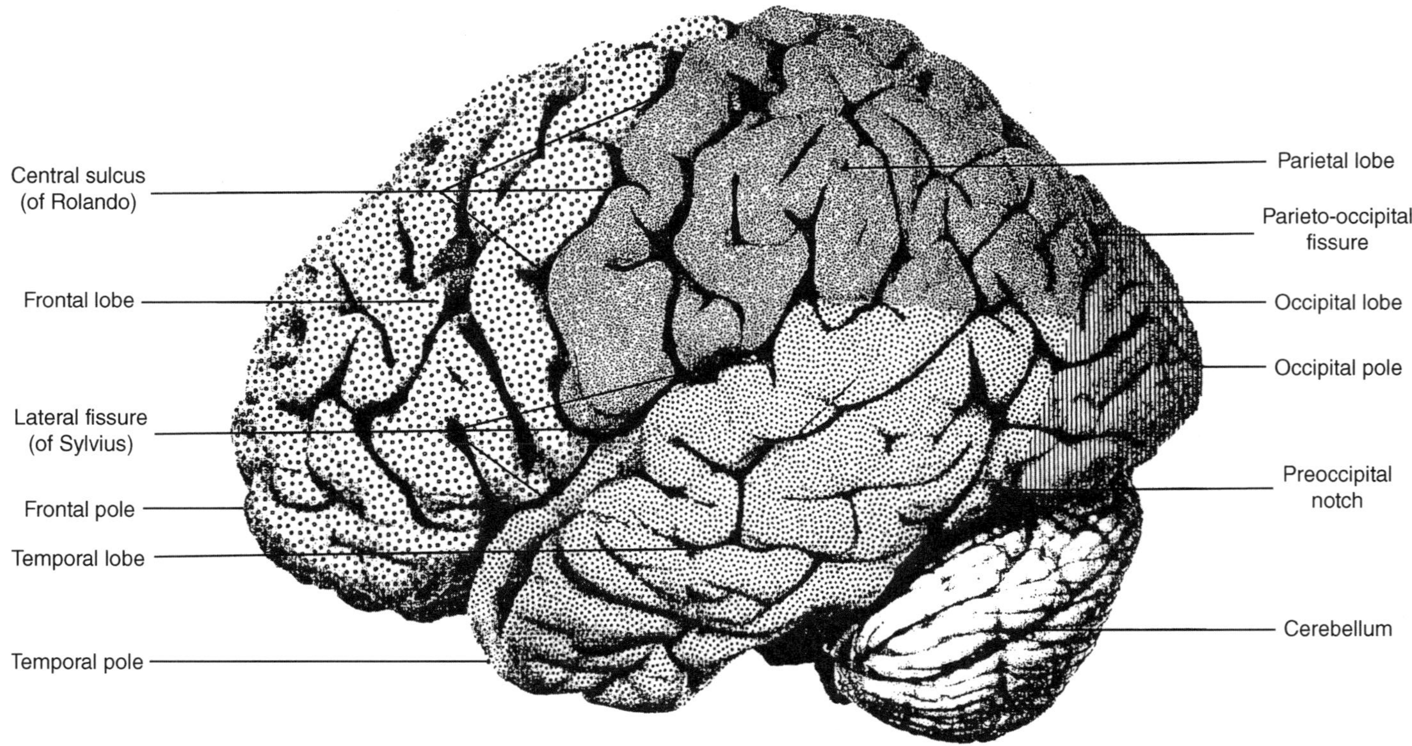

FIGURE 1 Lateral view of the brain demonstrating the various lobes of the hemisphere.

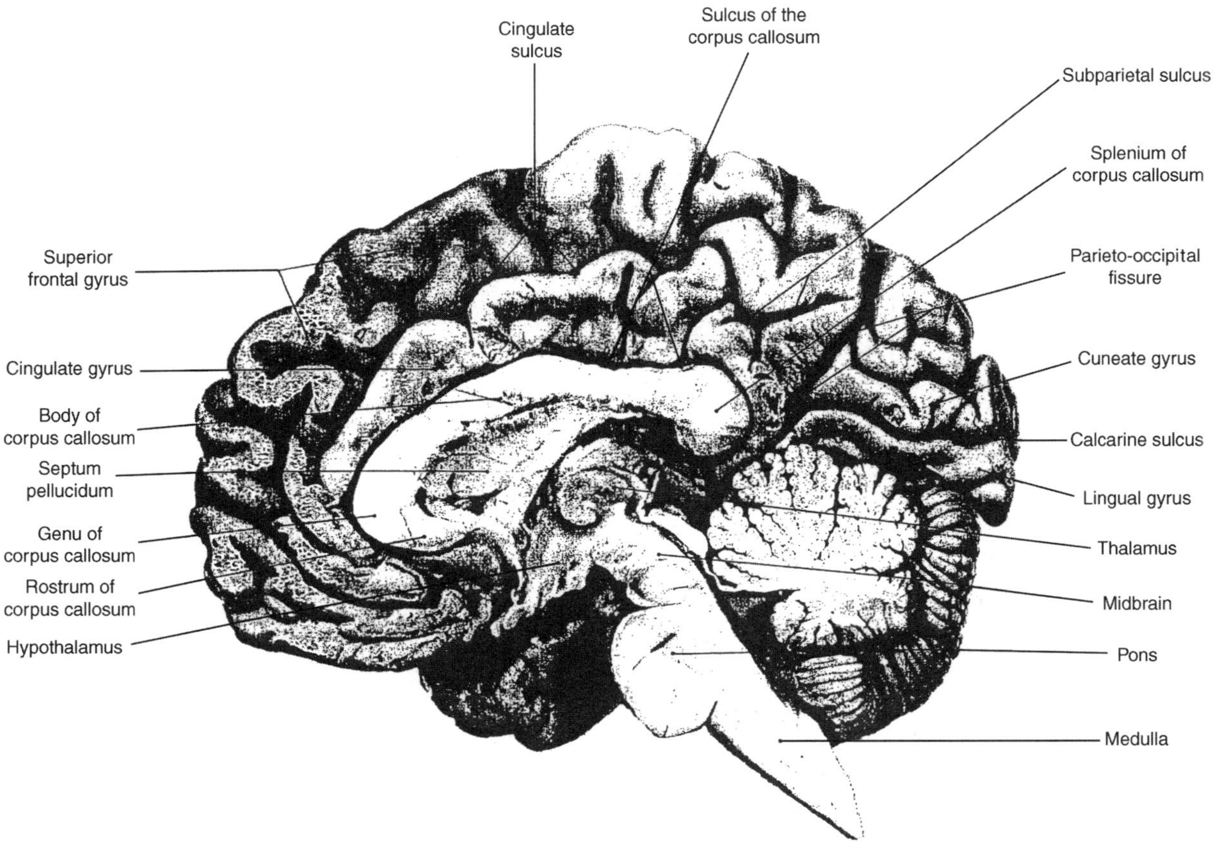

FIGURE 2 Medial view of the right half of a brain sectioned in the sagittal plane to demonstrate the gyri and sulci on the medial surface of the hemisphere.

Parietal Lobe Damage (Varies by Left Versus Right Hemisphere)

Changes in sensation and perception of touch, pain, temperature, body position in space, and vibration
Problems with integration of sensory-perceptual information
Difficulty seeing "the big picture" or the gestalt
Problems with reading and arithmetic
Trouble with mechanical, visual spatial, or tactual spatial tasks
Visual field disturbances, including inattention or neglect
Trouble with directions
Lack of awareness of deficits
Paranoia or misperception

Subcortical Injuries: Anoxia, Tumors, Stroke

Memory
Attention
Speed of information processing
Other difficulties depending on nature of damage and impact on connected structures

MOST COMMONLY CITED COGNITIVE DEFICITS AFTER TRAUMATIC BRAIN INJURY: A 20-YEAR REVIEW OF THE LITERATURE

Reduced attention and concentration
Heightened distractibility
Memory problems and reduced new learning capacity
Slowness in thinking and performance
Problems in flexibility of thinking
Difficulties with planning, organizing, and initiation
Reduced abstract reasoning capacity
Impaired complex information-processing skills
Problems in judgment
Visual spatial and visual perceptual impairments (e.g., directions, path finding, mechanical skills, location of objects in space, Hemi-inattention
Low fatigue threshold
Communication disturbances, including verbal expansiveness and tangentiality
Basic intellectual deficits as measured by IQ
Confusion and perplexity

TOPIC: WHAT IS ATTENTION? WHAT IS MEMORY? HOW DO THEY WORK IN REAL LIFE?

Pay Attention

Most of the time we need to pay attention to things in our life. We may listen to an important newsflash; we may look at a landmark to find our way; we may even need to listen to and look at something at the same time.

Paying attention to someone or something may help us recall it at a later time.

We Use Different Kinds of Attention

We use different kinds of attention. We *sustain* attention while watching TV, reading, or writing a letter.

Sometimes we need to "tune out" distracting noises by *selectively attending* to reading the newspaper. Daily we *shift* attention from one thing to another. For example, doing a variety of house chores (laundry, dishes, gardening) or *alternating* between reading a recipe and getting out ingredients. Some people can *divide* their attention between two or three things at the same time. For example, talking on the phone while watching TV.

Ways to Aid Attention in Everyday Life

1. Reduce environmental noise, activity, and distractions.
2. Correct sensory losses (eyesight, hearing).
3. Make sure the room is well lit.
4. Maintain consistent exercise program (20–30 minutes, three times a week)
5. Participate in activities that stimulate thinking.
6. Use compensations, for example
   a. Highlight key words when reading.
   b. Ask someone to slow down if they are talking too fast.
   c. Ask someone to repeat information.
   d. Take written notes.
   e. Paraphrase information you hear for clarification.
7. Pay attention to the environment, note key landmarks on your route.
8. You may have to change focus and tell yourself "I'm doing this now."
9. Save difficult tasks for your optimal times of focus and thinking.
10. Meditation—to reduce internal distractions.

Pleasurable Activities to Stimulate Attention

1. Board games (Scrabble, Cribbage, Monopoly)
2. Walking or exercise
3. Crossword puzzles
4. Knitting or crocheting
5. Playing cards (solitaire, gin rummy, bridge)
6. Reading
7. Putting together photo albums

We Use Different Kinds of Memory

People can often recall where they were born or the name of their first-grade teacher, but have trouble remembering what they had for breakfast. It's often easy to forget to "remember to remember" to do something or to tell someone something important.

Long-term memory is the well-learned information store; *short-term memory* is information kept 30 minutes to a day or two; *immediate memory* is information held for the moment (e.g., looking up a phone number), and *prospective memory* is remembering to remember to do something.

Ways to Aid Memory in Everyday Life

1. Use external memory aids: clock, alarm, calendar, daily planner, lists.
2. Daily planner
   a. Plan the day.
   b. Open book before activity.
   c. Write in during or after activity.
   d. Review and summarize day.
3. Mnemonics—most effective when recalling lists or unrelated items.
   a. Imagery of name (Dr. Fordyce: imagine four dice in a white coat).
   b. Alphabet cueing—first letter cueing to recall street names in Seattle ("Jesus Christ Made Seattle Under Pressure." J=James, Jefferson; C=Cherry, Columbia; M=Marion, Madison; S=Spring, Seneca; U = Union, University; P=Pine, Pike).
   c. PQRST (Preview, question, read, summarize, test)
4. Organize information—break things down into steps.

Further Notes on Memory for Cognitive Group

It can be helpful to think of MEMORY as a three stage process

Stage I: Acquisition of New Information

When you are trying to first absorb new information, you need to do the following:

a. Understand what is being said or shown.
b. Focus and sustain your concentration.
c. Juggle several ideas in your mind at once.
d. Avoid distractions or being pulled off task.
e. Think quickly.

Stage II: Storage of New Information

In order for information to be most effectively stored, it must be

a. Repeated
b. Rehearsed or practiced in several ways (e.g., written down, discussed)
c. Organized
d. Summarized in main ideas or key words or symbols
e. Linked to something *meaningful*, or made meaningful to you

Stage III: Retrieval of New Information after a Delay

To maximize the chances that stored information will pop into mind when needed, it helps to do the following:

a. Make effective use of cues (e.g., a reminder posted in obvious spot).
b. Take good notes, using main ideas and key words.
c. Get in the habit of reviewing your notes throughout the day—this improves the chances for spontaneous recall later.
d. Use daily, weekly, and monthly routines and consistency of habits to free up mental energy for recall.
e. Leave critical items in a single, consistent location (e.g., keys, cell phone, Daytimer).

STRATEGIES FOR MEMORY ENHANCEMENT AND RETENTION

Internal Strategies

1. Auditory rehearsal (silent)
2. Auditory repetition (aloud)
3. Mnemonics
4. Chunking
5. Associations
   a. Associated movements—"When I snap my fingers I need my meds."

   b. Associated movement patterns—"When I close the door I turn the lock."
   c. Associated movement triggers—"When I brush my teeth I take my meds."
6. Visual imagery
   Pictures of auditory input, semantic images, absurd images

External Strategies

1. Memory book
2. Alarm
3. Post-it notes

Important Principles to Remember

1. Practice
2. Make it automatic
3. Overlearning—Keep practicing even after you get it.
4. Organization—specific sequence—the same way
5. Change to own words to use working memory to aid retention.
6. Involve patient in defining strategies to find out what they like best.

Short-Term Memory Strategies

1. **Repetition:** This is a good method to remember things for short periods of time. For example, if you call Information for a phone number, but do not have a pen, you can repeat the number over and over in your mind until you dial it. There is another form of repetition that does store information over and over for several days, so you begin to remember all or, at least, part of it. Repetition is especially good for remembering new names. When you meet someone new, try to say their name aloud several times. "Nice to meet you, Julie." "I have a cousin named Julie." The more you actively use that name the better chance you have stored that name in your memory and can recall it later.

2. **Association:** Associate a new piece of information with an old piece of previously learned information. If you meet someone with the same last name as an old friend, associate that new person with the old friend. A person may have a name that sounds like an object. Try to associate the name with the object (i.e., John Beasley—try to imagine John with a bee flying around his head).

3. **Visualization:** Make a picture in your mind. This method is effective for routes or locations. Picture yourself getting from place to place, or see yourself sitting in the doctor's office with a clock above your head showing the appointment time.

4. **Adjust your routine and environment:**
   a. Keep a calendar or appointment book where all appointments are written. You will need to check your calendar or appointment book in a very systematic fashion. One way is to check the calendar in the morning, lunchtime, evening, and right before you go to bed. If this is not enough, check it on an hourly basis. After every significant task is completed, check it off. It is also a good to review those days that have passed to gain perspective on the passage of time.
   b. It is also helpful to keep a journal or diary of the day's events and how you were feeling and doing with your memory on a specific day. Once something is written down, you can always refer back to it.
   c. Try to keep all important articles (wallet, keys, checkbook, glasses, medicine) in the same place. Things will be much easier to locate quickly.

GENERAL RULES OF GOOD COMMUNICATION

1. Eye contact—Regular but not unflinching!
2. Not interrupting. Let the other person finish.
3. Taking turns.
4. Avoid abrupt topic shifts.
5. Beware of being too self-referenced.
   a. Ask other person questions about themselves.
   b. Make sympathetic comments.
6. Be aware that fatigue can lead to communication problems.
7. Try to speak clearly.
8. Avoid monotone; use expression in voice.
9. Respect personal space—3 feet.
10. Be a good listener (eye contact, head nod, feedback).
11. Check in with listener or speaker.
12. Be aware of listener—do they have something to say?
    a. body language
    b. verbal interruptions ("um," "ah," "humph!")
13. Be open to related topics with smooth topic transitions.

TIME-MANAGEMENT STRATEGIES

I. Getting ready to leave the house
   A. Plan ahead the night before.
      1. Gather things you will need.

2. Plan how you will get there and time you will leave.
3. Plan route and travel time.
4. Plan or estimate how long it will take to get ready and write out a checklist.
    a. Bathe or shower
    b. Dressed
    c. Eating and taking meds
5. Pick out clothes the night before.
6. Go set alarm immediately after determining the time you need to get up.
7. Go to bed at a decent hour.
8. Do evening check of Daytimer.
9. Check gas tank.

B. That morning
1. Get up at planned time.
2. Follow your set routine.
3. Avoid distractions.
    a. Don't take phone calls.
    b. Don't start new projects (cleaning, organization, etc.).
    c. Don't fuss too much (with appearance).
    d. Be aware of time with newspaper, TV, Internet.
    e. Pets and playtime at end of day.
    f. Avoid lengthy discussions with family.
4. Review daily schedule.
5. Set an alarm if napping before you leave house.
6. Double check items to bring.
7. Double check that house is secured.
8. Make checklist for items you need to always do or have with you before you leave and post a checklist in a prominent place.
9. Try to leave the same time each day.

II. Completing projects

A. Be aware of due dates.
B. Schedule time and stick to it.
C. List steps in projects.
D. Gather materials you need before starting.
E. Pace yourself and schedule breaks.
F. Avoid distractions.
G. If possible, match your energy to task complexity (i.e., try to do complex tasks at your optimal time of day).
H. If task order is critical, stick to that rather than matching complexity to energy.
I. Control your environment.

J. Estimate time to complete each step and review and revise estimates periodically.
K. Review steps and plans periodically.

III. Fatigue
A. Be aware of best time of day.
B. Know your endurance limits (how long can you work without a break).
C. Work efficiently. Notice when fatigue decreases performance (e.g., mistakes increase and train of thought decreases, sensitivity to distractions increases).
D. Sleep needs change after brain injury.
E. Regular meals help fatigue—avoid being famished and eat healthy.
F. Adjust schedule on "bad days" (e.g., ill, overtired, stress, or no real reason, etc.).
G. Exercise is helpful.
H. Do at least one pleasant event or activity per day.

PLANNING AND ORGANIZING

Planning

Different activities require different types of planning to make them happen successfully. The following are three basic types of activities and strategies for planning them effectively.

I. Schedule
A. The goal of planning your schedule is to have a clear daily list of obligations and tasks that include the following:
1. Routines
2. Intermittent variables
3. Open slots

B. What are the components of a schedule that need to be planned?
1. Classes
2. Appointments
3. Work
4. Chores and errands
5. Meetings
6. Phone calls
7. Exercise
8. Social/fun
9. Transportation
10. Vacation
11. Medications

12. Other family members activities
13. Sleep/wake

C. Tips for effective planning of schedule
1. Consistent time to plan schedule
2. Consistent review of schedule
3. Have a good system that works for you
4. Allow for down time
5. Allow for extra time between activities
6. Space for "to do" list
7. Place for phone numbers and addresses is helpful

II. Projects (use ABODES system)
A. Organize your office
B. Clean out the garage

III. Events/activities (use ABODES system)
A. Plan a vacation trip
B. Plan a dinner party

ABODES

Organization

A Assess the situation
B Break into steps
O Order the steps
D Decide what is needed
E Estimate time
S Survey the work

*A*ssess the situation (i.e. who, what, where, when, etc.)

____

____

____

____

____

____

____

*B*reak into steps *O*rder steps

1. ____

2. ____

3. ____________________
4. ____________________
5. ____________________
6. ____________________
7. ____________________
8. ____________________
9. ____________________
10. ____________________

*D*ecide what is needed (i.e. supplies, tools, forms, clothes)

1. ____________________
2. ____________________
3. ____________________
4. ____________________
5. ____________________
6. ____________________

*E*stimate time needed to complete (use day timer or memory book to schedule steps and time to get the material needed)

____

____

____

____

____

*S*urvey the work

Is each step completed?
Does the finished product look like what you planned?
Is the finished product what you intended?

If your plan is not working:

- Be flexible
- Change the order of the steps
- Look for alternative solutions

NOTE TAKING STRATEGIES (COGNITIVE GROUP)

Taking notes is an important skill to help improve ability to remember and follow through with day to day activities.

When to take notes:

- New information
- Appointments/scheduled activities
- To organize information
- ______________________________
- ______________________________

Taking notes for appointments/activities

- Date and time
- Who it is with
- What it is about
- Location
- Purpose of appointment/meeting

Taking notes with new/important information

- Get the main idea
- Use an outline format
- Be prepared
- Use key words, abbreviations, symbols
- Review and revise notes promptly after class/meeting
- Ask questions to clarify meaning
- Slow speaker down
- Leave spaces between lines to add information later if necessary
- Use tape recorder if possible
- Compare notes with someone else in the class
- ______________________________
- ______________________________
- ______________________________
- ______________________________

APPENDIX K

BUSINESS DEDUCTIONS TO TRACK FOR TAX PURPOSES

(*NOTE*: Check with your own accountant or legal advisor for the final word on deductions appropriate to your practice)

DIRECT EXPENSES

Office rent
Office phones
Furniture
Equipment, including computer, FAX, tests
Supplies, including testing protocols, stationery, office supplies
Contract labor, including psychometrists, secretary, billing help
Professional dues
Books, journals
Postage
Marketing expenses
Cleaning expenses
Malpractice insurance
Cost of license
Travel miles to office
Travel to professional meetings
Conference costs

INDIRECT OR OTHER EXPENSES

Use of office in home: You may be able to deduct a percentage of your household expenses (based upon total square footage of your home used exclusively for work-related duties, such as scheduling, dictation, etc.). You may deduct this corresponding percentage of household utilities, repairs, maintenance, lawn and garden maintenance, and other household maintenance costs as part of your business expense.

Find a good accountant who is familiar with psychology practices.

APPENDIX L

REVIEW OF THE MENTAL STATUS EXAM - BY MARY PEPPING, PH.D.

1. **Appearance**: pt's dress, grooming, carriage, facial expressions and eye contact, mannerisms, and any unusual movements.

2. **Orientation**: appreciation of time, place, person, and present situation; sometimes include pt's awareness of examiner's role

3. **Speech**: observations are made of both **delivery** (deviations from normal rate, tone quality, articulation, phrasing, smoothness and ease of delivery) and **content** (misuse or confusion of words, grammatical and syntactical errors, perseverations, dysnomia, and other deficits in word production & organization.

4. **Thinking**: mental confusion, quality and appropriateness of associations, logic, clarity, coherence, rate of thought production, blocking, confabulation, circumstantiality, rationalization (assuming pts are not aphasic, verbally dyspraxic, or so profoundly vegetatively depressed as to be almost mute), these aspects of thinking can be surveyed, and distinguished from speech per se

5. **Attention, concentration and memory**: span of attention, recent, and remote history, asking for names, dates, places and events, along with digit span, and recall of three or four words. Serial sevens and digits in reverse are standard MSE concentration tasks

6. **Intellectual functioning**: examination of general intellectual functioning is based on quality of vocabulary, reasoning, judgment, and organization of thought as well as answers to questions about topics of general information, fairly simple arithmetic problems, and abstract reasoning tasks. e.g. proverbs, similarities, simple drawing (clock) and copying (cubes, overlapping pentagrams), and brief assessment of reading and writing

7. **Emotional state**: both **mood** (the pt's prevailing emotional tone) and **affect** (the range of appropriateness of emotional responses) need to be distinguished and reported. Mood constitutes the "ground" and affect the "figure" of the pt.'s emotional behavior.

8. **Special preoccupations and experiences**: the examiner looks for reports or expressions of bodily concerns, distortions of self concept, obsessional tendencies, phobias, paranoid ideation, suicidal thoughts, delusions, hallucinations, and strange experiences such as dissociation, fugue states, feelings of impersonalization or unreality.

9. **Insight**: based upon an evaluation of the pt.'s self understanding, appreciation of her or his condition, and his/her expectations and plans.

APPENDIX M

INTERVIEW FORMAT

Reason for being here, in patient's own words: I usually tell the patient I have had the chance to review their medical file, but I always like to hear directly from them, why they are here to see me today. I thank family member for coming, and let them know I will ask for their input after the patient has first answered.

Areas of difficulty *as volunteered* by the patient: Obtain their spontaneous list of concerns first, then ask your own questions regarding:

Cognitive problems or concerns
Physical problems
Mood related changes or emotional concerns as well as any personality change
Impact of problems on Activities of Daily Living and upon job/work performance

Medical History: Previous loss of consciousness, duration, other serious blows to the head

Prior serious accidents or injuries
Falls; sports accidents
Motor vehicle accidents
Premorbid history of convulsions or seizures
Current seizure activity and anticonvulsant medications
High fevers – greater than 104 degrees
Heat stroke
Near drowning with loss of consciousness or resuscitation
Toxic exposures, such as lead, solvents, heavy metals
Meningitis, encephalitis, scarlet fever, rheumatic fever, tuberculosis, AIDS
Past surgeries
Menstrual or hormonal problems

Other significant medical problems (e.g. cancer, heart disease or MI)
Cause of death for parents if deceased
Parental health problems, if parents are living
Alzheimer's disease history in family
Family history of migraine headache, hypertension, or other illnesses
Personal or family history of learning disability or Attention Deficit Disorder
Obtain an updated list of patients current medications – check first with patient, to see if he or she knows their own medications and dosages.
Sensory issues: are there problems with vision or hearing? Do these predate the current medical problems, or are they directly related, or are they coincidental changes?
Has the patient undergone any inpatient or outpatient rehabilitation treatment?

Personal and Social History Birth and Development – was patient a full term baby? Any problems at birth? Did they learn to walk and talk at typical points in their development? Typical childhood illnesses?

School years – strengths and weaknesses
Highest grade achieved and grade point average in high school or college.
Siblings and Parents – ages, occupations and marital status
Marital Status of patient
Children/Grandchildren – general health and well-being
Occupational History
Military Service and Discharge status, i.e., honorable, general, or dishonorable
Leisure time pursuits

Psychiatric History Is there a biological family history of psychiatric problems or treatment, including psychiatric hospitalization, electroconvulsive treatment, and/or psychotropic medications?

Family history of alcohol or drug abuse
For the patient:
Psychiatric hospitalizations
History of suicide attempts
History of ECT
Physical or sexual abuse
Verbal or emotional abuse
Any history of post-traumatic stress disorder?
Any diagnoses such as fibromyalgia or chronic fatigue syndrome?
Previous psychotherapy? Dates and types

Psychotropic medications in past or present
Outpatient treatment for depression, anxiety

Current Psychological Status Make note of typical **mental status exam** features, including the patient's affect, mood, anxiety, depression, panic disorder, psychosis, thought disorder, hallucinations or delusions, ideas of reference, depersonalization
Vegetative Issues Sleep, appetite, weight gain or loss, changes in libido and sexual function, energy level, loss of interest or pleasure in usual activities
Current and Past Substance Use

Alcohol
Marijuana, Cocaine, Amphetamines, Hallucinogens
Pain meds, other prescription medications
Non-prescription medications
Use of Nicotine–Caffeine

History of Legal Problems or Arrests

Has the patient ever been arrested for a felony?
Have they served time in jail or prison?

Does the patient currently have an attorney?
Is there a legal case pending?
What is the patient's typical day now – Normal routine and activities?
What was their pre-morbid work or school schedule?
What does the patient or family hope to gain from the evaluation?
Anything I haven't asked you that you would like to tell me?

APPENDIX N

Some questions cannot be accurately answered by the results of neuropsychological evaluation or intervention. Common questions and issues:

SAMPLE PATIENT QUESTIONS:

Question: "I have had three concussions in the last several years – which one of them caused the problems I am having now?"
Issue: There is no way to definitively sort out which concussion caused which impairments, or the relative degree of them.
Question: "I want to be able to recall what happened at the time of my accident. Can therapy help me recover my memories?"
Issue: There is no way to know if the information recalled is an accurate memory of events, or if it is a remnant of a dream, something the patient read or heard, information presented on a TV show, or some other non-verifiable source of what the patient now feels is a true memory. Without accurate and independent external corroboration of facts, recovered memories are always suspect.

SAMPLE PROVIDER QUESTIONS:

Question: "This patient has a history of chronic alcoholism and serious drug abuse, along with a couple of head injuries, and a learning disability before all of this happened. Can you help us determine which of the current deficits are related to each concern?"
Issue: Too many potentially overlapping types and sources of cognitive difficulty.
Question: "Can't you just do a memory test, and let us know if the patient's memory function is normal or not?"

Issue: There is no way to determine if the resulting score, in isolation, is "normal" for this particular patient, or if the score is a sign of early decline or change as the result of an injury. More information is needed about the patient's overall intellectual skills and other areas of function to put the memory performances in a larger and more accurate context. While a 40th percentile score may be technically within normal limits, it may represent a significant change for this person. You would not be able to determine this solely on the basis of information about their age and education.

APPENDIX O

MARKETING LETTER SAMPLES

THE "TOO GENERAL" LETTER:

Dear Dr. Jones:

I have recently opened a neuropsychological practice in this area, and I would be happy to assist with evaluations for any of your adult patients with neurologic problems that might affect brain function. I see adolescents and adults who are ages 16 and above.

Please feel free to contact me if you have any questions about my services. I have enclosed a card for future reference and would be happy to speak with you.

Sincerely,
Neuropsychologist, Ph.D.

APPENDIX P

MARKETING LETTER SAMPLES

THE BETTER LETTER:

Dear Dr. Jones:

I have recently opened a neuropsychological practice in this area, and I hope to have the opportunity to speak with you and your colleagues about services that may be helpful to your patients and practice.

My primary areas of work have included evaluation and treatment of patients ages 16 and above who have suffered traumatic brain injury, multiple sclerosis, brain tumors, anoxic injuries or dementing conditions. The focus of evaluation for these patients has been to identify residual cognitive and neurobehavioral abilities and deficits and to provide specific treatment recommendations or clarify diagnostic questions.

I have enclosed a copy of my vitae for more detailed information about my training and experience. I would also be very happy to give a formal presentation to your group on the nature and clinical utility of neuropsychological evaluations, or upon a specific patient group of interest.

I will plan to call you next week to see if we might meet, and if a presentation from me is something that might be agreeable to you and your staff. In the meantime, please feel free to contact me directly if you have any questions.

Sincerely. . . .

INDEX